WALLACE STEVENS

and the Symbolist Imagination

The Orbit of Thomas Mann. By Erich Kahler

*On Four Modern Humanists:
Hofmannsthal, Gundolf, Curtius, Kantorowicz.
Edited by Arthur R. Evans, Jr.*

*Flaubert and Joyce:
The Rite of Fiction. By Richard K. Cross*

*A Stage for Poets:
Studies in the Theatre of Hugo and Musset.
By Charles Affron*

Hofmannsthal's Novel Andreas. By David H. Miles

*On Gide's Prométhée: Private Myth
and Public Mystification. By Kurt Weinberg*

*Kazantzakis and the Linguistic Revolution
in Greek Literature. By Peter Bien*

*Wallace Stevens and the Symbolist Imagination.
By Michel Benamou*

WALLACE STEVENS

and the Symbolist Imagination

BY MICHEL BENAMOU

PRINCETON UNIVERSITY PRESS 1972

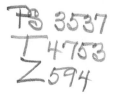

Copyright © 1972 by Princeton University Press
All rights reserved
LCC: 77-37574
ISBN: 0-691-06225-0

Printed in the United States of America by
Princeton University Press, Princeton, New Jersey
This book has been composed in Electra

Publication of this book has been aided by
the Whitney Darrow Publication Reserve Fund
of Princeton University Press

Acknowledgments

I AM GRATEFUL to the editors under whose copyrights my essays first appeared or were reprinted, and who granted permission to publish them here in the same or a modified version:

1 "Poetry and Painting," originally "Wallace Stevens: Some Relations Between Poetry and Painting" in *Comparative Literature*, XI (Winter 1959) reprinted in Brown and Haller, eds., *The Achievement of Wallace Stevens*, Lippincott 1962, was first delivered as a paper at the English Institute, Columbia University, on the invitation of Samuel French Morse.

2 "Jules Laforgue," originally "Jules Laforgue and Wallace Stevens; in *Romanic Review*, L (April 1959).

3 "Baudelaire and Mallarmé" originated as "Sur le prétendu symbolisme de Wallace Stevens," in *Critique*, XVII (Décembre 1961). It was expanded in English as "Wallace Stevens and the Symbolist Imagination," *E.L.H.* XXXI (March 1964) and reprinted in Pearce and Miller, eds., *The Act of the Mind*, Johns Hopkins, 1965.

4 "Apollinaire," originally "Apollinaire and Wallace Stevens," in *Comparative Literature* (Fall 1968), was a paper read at a Midwest Modern Language Association cochaired by Prof. Robert J. Niess.

5 "Poetry and Alchemy" is expanded from "The Structures of Stevens' Imagination," in *Mundus Artium*, I (Winter 1966), a translation of a lecture sponsored by the University of Bordeaux at the bidding of Professors Béranger and Mane.

Contents

Abbreviations

For Wallace Stevens' works we follow this code:

C.P.   *The Collected Poems of Wallace Stevens*, 1955

L.W.S. *Letters of Wallace Stevens*, edited by Holly Stevens, 1966

N.A.   *The Necessary Angel*, 1951

O.P.   *Opus Posthumous*, edited, with an introduction, by Samuel French Morse, 1957

Introduction

Symbolic, Symbolist, and *Symboliste* are not, as Edward Engelberg has remarked, synonymous words. His introduction to *The Symbolist Poem* makes the point quite clearly. A Symbolist poem can exist apart from a symbolic system because it is usually a short lyric expressing in self-sufficient terms a private sensibility. Thus to Engelberg Yeats was a symbolic poet, Swinburne was a true Symbolist, and Stevens "a direct descendant of the French *Symbolistes*," by which he meant Baudelaire, Mallarmé, Laforgue. Possibly, we should adopt "symbolist(e)" as a temporary compromise, to include the double lineage, American and French, which ends in Stevens. The spelling would draw attention to the parenthetical nature of the French influence, and invite a question about the very idea of literary genealogies.

The word "imagination" further complicates thinking about Wallace Stevens. He used it liberally—some forty times in the poems, not to mention his lectures and essays. He hymned *the* imagination: high, capable, mighty, august, and above all, central, that is to say, man-centered. If there exists a central imagination in his poetry, then we should find it by comparing his images with other poets' images, but not necessarily American poets, and by comparing them with other phenomena of the imagination, such as art, but not necessarily by painters who were his contemporaries. Neither time nor space matters to the comparatist. Comparison at once implies a difference in the objects compared and the sameness of their maker, man. Stevens took that sameness for granted when he wrote in "Imagination as Value":

> The imagination that is satisfied by politics, whatever the
> nature of the politics, has not the same value as the imag-
> ination that seeks to satisfy, say, the *universal* mind,
> which, in the case of a poet, would be the imagination
> that tries to penetrate to *basic* images, *basic* emotions, and
> so to compose a *fundamental* poetry even older than the
> ancient world."[1]

It is easy to succumb, with Stevens, to what I shall briefly
call the anthropological temptation: on the one hand, poli-
tics and history; on the other, poetry and anthropology. For
a long time historical man monopolized the intellectual
stage. Anthropological man has become just as central, a
fetish of great usefulness to desacralize history as a system
of determination. But perhaps, as Roland Barthes once re-
marked, it is equally illusionistic.[2] For what evidence, except
anthropological, do we have to vouch for a "central man,"
"basic images," "basic emotions," a "universal mind," and a
"fundamental poetry"—in short, a guaranteed human norm?
An act of poetic faith is required of us if we want to speak
validly about the imagination. The idea of man's being a po-
etic fiction, the "supreme fiction," in Stevens' and Mallarmé's
wording, is central because it is poetic and poetic because
it is central. It may well be that the poetry of Wallace
Stevens is the supreme expression of the centrality of man,
and that his quest for centrality was already doomed by the
time some ethnologists (Lévi-Strauss, chiefly) set out to
discover a basic man "older than the ancient world" but

[1] N.A., p. 145.
[2] In *Théorie d'ensemble*, Paris, 1968, p. 27, n. 1.

present forever in a "universal mind." Poets and anthropologists share the same nostalgia for origins, for a center.[3] Today new kinds of writing attempt to break out of the nostalgic circle, by rending the symbolic system, unseating anthropological man from his central position. New kinds of criticism will have to follow suit. But, for the time being, reservations about a central imagination apply to the whole culture in which both Stevens and his critics originate. Stevens and the Symbolist imagination are one, if by symbolist we mean central, and by imagination a horizon of basic images the center of which has shifted, since ancient times, from god to man.

The attitude of the Symbolists toward symbols is itself ambiguous. As Cassirer suggestively wrote in *Language and Myth*, "All symbolism harbors the curse of mediacy." Symbols block man's access to reality. Whatever the status, human or divine, of reality, God or the unconscious appear veiled in images which idolaters adore and iconoclasts tear down. Even Baudelaire, who sang ecstatically of a oneness with the world based on universal analogy, "as vast as night and light," reversed his love of "Correspondances" in a sonnet which amounts to a Symbolist's Black Mass, "Obsession":

> Comme tu me plairais, ô nuit, sans ces étoiles
> Dont la lumière parle un langage connu,
> Car je cherche le vide et le noir et le nu![4]
> (How I would love you, o night, without stars

---

[3] The structuralist hankers for a place of repose at the unstructured center of structures. See J. Derrida, *De la Grammatologie*, Paris, 1967.

[4] Baudelaire, *Œuvres*, Paris, Gallimard, 1954, p. 147.

> Whose light speaks a well-known language,
> For I seek the bleak, the black, and the naked!)

This reversal is the start of the long descent into the image-less void which was to end with "le Voyage," Baudelaire's cry for deliverance from the imagination. Proscribing the very symbols he had worshipped, the idolater had turned iconoclast.

By a similar transformation, light in darkness symbolizing the imagination, Mallarmé began his poetic career under the spell of the moon (the poem "Apparition") but in mid-course wished for a chemical that would dissolve it out of the sky.[5] His quest of negativity and nakedness almost victoriously did away with symbols, at least as signs capable of revealing a hidden reality. Since language had failed him in its task of representing things materially, Mallarmé opted for silence. Light would come from the reciprocal fires of words across the gaps between them, so that syntax perhaps would remedy the meaninglessness of words taken separately. God alone wrote luminously on a dark field with the alphabet of stars.[6] Man's ink was black and the page white. His was not the language of stars in the night sky. Eventually the poem would renounce all symbolic function, any outside reality it could symbolize, for with enough luck it might become a constellation ("rien . . . excepté . . . peut-être . . . une constellation").[7] Man would make a sky of his own. The typographical experiments of *Le Coup de dés* and the page permutations of *Le Livre* thus tended to deny

[5] Letter from Mallarmé to François Coppée, 18 July 1872.

[6] Mallarmé, *Œuvres Complètes*, Paris, 1961, p. 370.

[7] *Ibid.*, p. 474-477.

primacy to symbols and metaphors: the spacing of words alone would create new and strange music. Mallarmé's ambition to rival music with words has been much misunderstood: music for him meant neither euphony nor evocation but structure.[8] It was a way of dispensing with symbols.

Although Mallarmé's *no* to reality differed from Stevens' *yes*, and a vast difference it is, the two poets at least shared the self-conscious attitude of the Symbolist about the fictive nature of poetry. For exactly opposite purposes Stevens and Mallarmé sought a poetry "untouched by trope or deviation":[9] Mallarmé because he despaired of transposing the world materially into words, Stevens because he hoped to return to the real—"straight to the object. . . . At the exactest point at which it is itself." But is it not paradoxical that the two poets clothed in the same metaphor their diverging quests for immediacy, and that they equated symbols with coverings (Mallarmé's feathers, scales, make-up, Stevens' hats, leaves, varnish) and immediacy with nakedness? I explore this paradox at some length in the essay on Stevens and the Symbolist imagination from which this collection takes its title. The iconoclastic aspect of Symbolism merits attention. To Mallarmé's "comme si" repeated in *Le Coup de dés* corresponds Stevens' "as if," by which the poet seemed to remind himself that symbols are not to be confused with things as they are.

In short, three concerns have accompanied the comparatist in his long itinerary with Wallace Stevens: the question of

---

[8] Jean-Pierre Richard, *L'Univers Imaginaire de Mallarmé*, Paris, 1961, p. 415.
[9] *C.P.*, p. 471.

the French influence, the problem of a universal imagina-
tion, and the ambiguous status of symbols within Symbolism
itself. Allow me now to turn from generalities to specifics.

The following essays were written over the past fifteen
years. Only the last one has undergone substantial changes;
the other four remain exactly as they appeared in journals,
except for a word here and there changed at the suggestion
of Stevens critics, several of whom have honored me by
remarks in their books—notably Joseph N. Riddel, Frank
Doggett, and Robert Buttel. In the act of collecting these
essays I shall attempt to collect myself, and to define the
scope, the method, the spirit of literary comparison.

Rather than his ostensible Frenchness, it was Stevens'
universal quality which first attracted me to him. It was in
1955 at the American Library in Paris. Stevens had just
died. I chanced upon "Asides on the Oboe," written in
1940. In this poem an American poet fought against war
hysteria and found peace in the metaphor, enticingly philo-
sophical to a young Frenchman, of a planetary man, a
human globe, "the glass man without external references."
We are today, more than thirty years later, increasingly
aware of the fictive, not to say fictitious, nature of the
belief in a central man. Yet if the study of this idea of man,
by necessity comparative, should reinforce the oneness of
man's creations, it might still provide us with the best
kind of objectivity, and therefore sanity, that is available to
us. This "passionate objectivity," different from the cold
neutrality of science, elevates criticism above what René
Wellek called "the customs house theory of literature," an
import-export balance sheet favorable to national pride. I
am not a Frenchman engaged in computing Stevens' debt

to France in order to settle an old account with Poe, nor do I seek to ingratiate myself with departments of Yankee literature by discounting the *symboliste* contraband smuggled in the baggage of an Imagist. Rather, I have hoped to reach, below surface resemblances and divergences of theme and style, to the common motives of the symbolic process which, if they exist, will allow us to compare a picture by Hokusai or Monet and a poem by Rilke or Stevens; I said "if they exist" because unless they exist comparative literature will not be able to transgress national boundaries. Beyond the privileged works of art which we compare, there must exist the common imaginative needs of men everywhere.

And so a shift from nationalistic to universal values in literary criticism also means a shift from positivistic to structural methods of interpretation. The positivistic demands documented proof of one writer's influence on another. For instance René Taupin, whose major study, *L'influence du Symbolisme français sur la poésie américaine* (1910-1920), gave a methodological model for comparatists in 1929, asked Wallace Stevens about a French influence and received the following confirmation:

> La légèreté, la grâce, le son et la couleur du français ont eu sur moi une influence indéniable et une influence précieuse (p. 276).

Two decades later, another scholar in search of proof elicited this by no means less evasive response:

> I have read something, more or less, of all the poets mentioned by you [Mallarmé, Verlaine, Laforgue, Valéry, & Baudelaire], but if I have picked up anything from

them, it has been unconsciously. It is always possible that where a man's attitude coincides with your own attitude, or accentuates your own attitude, you get a great deal from it without effort (To Hi Simons, L.W.S. 361).

The slight discrepancy between the 1919 admission and the 1941 disclaimer suggests several possibilities. If on the one hand these letters are to be taken seriously, perhaps Stevens did move from a fascination with the painterly and musical qualities of French to a poetic attitude akin to that of the Symbolistes. But on the other hand why should critics take seriously letters poets write to them? It is not the fact of influence but the meaning of affinity that matters. The key term for us here is the word unconscious. On it hinges the opposition between positivistic and structuralist interpretation. For the positivist art is a conscious creation. Hence the hunt for sources and influences. The intention of a poem could be reduced to the intention of the poet if that intention were to be known with sufficient clarity. In a first step the hypothesis of influence is inferred from parallel themes and fragments such as an image or a motif. The second step of literary positivism consists in proving the relationship by biographical data. Finally a judgment is passed on the quality of the imitation.

On the contrary, the structuralist demands no proof. When he speaks about deep affinities between Stevens and the early Baudelaire, or compares Stevens' style in some phase with Impressionism and in another with Cubism, there are no documents, no conscious borrowings. Affinity is a matter of unconscious symbolical values which resonate,

at many levels, with the "great mythic writing in which man-
kind tries out its meanings, that is to say its desires"[10]—in
other words, with the symbolic imagination which traverses
the individual works of a specific time and makes them con-
temporaries of another time, however remote it may be. The
structuralist does not invoke a "world-view" or a "Zeitgeist"
to explain affinities, since that would mean that he gives as
an explanation that which needs to be explained. Uncon-
scious meanings can be interpreted by a science of the
unconscious, as desires and fears. An individual symbol func-
tions in a network of symbols, interrelated and forming
systems of binary oppositions, so that to ascribe it a mean-
ing separate from that of the total network is to mutilate
its meaning. One can prove the justness of a comparison only
by reintegrating into the structure to which it belongs each
motif, image, or symbol compared, and by comparing struc-
tures, not merely motifs, images, or symbols. The proof of
each part of the system derives from the truth of the whole
system. The whole truth is the truth of the whole, and no
amount of documented proof could excuse the structuralist
from risking the whole system of symbols on every indi-
vidual symbol he seeks to interpret. A personal example
will perhaps help to clarify this *circulus methodicus*.

Early critics of Stevens inferred an influence of the Sym-
bolist poet Jules Laforgue on Wallace Stevens from the
apparent likeness of their poetic hero dressed as Pierrot. In
addition, Stevens' moon, "mother of pathos and pity"
(C.P. 107) seemed to imitate the Laforguian deity of easeful

<hr>

[10] Roland Barthes, *Critique et Vérité*, Paris, 1966, p. 61.

death. But I felt that these parallels made no sense, as the second essay in this collection will maintain. The reason for the critical falsification that had occurred was that a separate theme was wrenched out of the fabric of Stevens' symbolic system. The moon certainly exerted the attraction of a death-wish on Laforgue's Pierrot, while Stevens' lunar phase was part of a spiritual conflict finally won by heroic feelings symbolized by the sun. The case, simply stated, of Pierrot *lunaire* versus solar hero, would be closed, both poets of course pleading no contest, except that in the process it revealed that the counterpart of Pierrot in *Harmonium*, Stevens' first collection of poems, was Hoon, the personification of his poetic self. The name has puzzled many readers; and anyone's guess, including Stevens' own as reader of his poems, seemed to me equally plausible and unconvincing,[11] until I tried a structural interpretation first of the poem and then of the place of the poem in *Harmonium*. The title, "Tea at the Palaz of Hoon," says directly this hero is a king, and he receives the three regal attributes of purple, ointment, and hymns. Power and central imagination, from the line "Out of my mind the golden ointment rained," are however abridged by the negative syntax: "Not less was I myself. . . ." Curiously enough the birth of this heroic figure is identified not with the rise of the sun, but with its descent.

[11] Delmore Schwarz read for Hoon "human alone," Marianne Moore "human," Stevens in an uncollected letter to William van O'Connor of March 31, 1949, wrote that he did not remember the origin of the word . . . "a mental abridgment possibly for who knows . . . everybody, more accurately anybody," and in a 1955 letter to Norman Holmes Pearson "probably an automatic cipher for "the loneliest air." (L.W.S. 871)

The difficulty of self-affirmation in the formula "not less myself" suggests the opposite of what it says. The poem negates its descensional imagery. Unlike most of the poems in *Harmonium*, which belong to a nocturnal imagination, Hoon tries to join the constellation of the sun which will dominate the following collections of verse. His name is the name of the hero who was being born in Stevens' poetry round 1921 by a painful process of individuation, which replaced the encroachment of the moon by a solar heroism. Is it not possible then that Stevens unconsciously replaced the maternal M of Moon with the heroic H of Hoon? A word-count showing the steady decline of the lunar motif and the corresponding rise of solar values places the poem at a turning point in Stevens' evolution. The sun-moon (animus-anima) conflict in the name Hoon would also explain why in "Sad Strains of a Gay Waltz" Hoon is "mountain-minded," an allusion not only to Stevens' lonely walks on Mount Penn, but symbolically to the solar constellation of height with light and sight. There was no comparable evolution in Laforgue's poetry.

I ventured earlier that comparison at once implies a difference in the things compared and the sameness of their maker, man. By that I meant a unity of the symbolic process perceived through the diversity of its products. But the mind boggles before the sheer number of theories of the imagination. Because man is both an individual rich in existential singularity and a social animal who inherits from all his forebears instincts and reflexes as well as cultural patterns to which he must conform, the study of symbols must take into account at least two systems of forces, on the one hand psycho-individual pulsions, and on the other socio-archetypal intimations. To separate the two systems into existential versus archetypal criticism would keep our philosophical house in order, but philosophical neatness may be reductive. I would certainly call Sartre's theory of images reductive, as it displays a tendency to limit the imagination to the role of a defective copy. At the other end of the spectrum, Jung's mysticism allowed him to ignore the social conflicts which pressed archetypes to the surface, or at least it allowed his readers to ignore the link between the imagination and history. A balance of intrication holds together the acts of perceiving the quotidian (economic depression, age, the pleasures of merely circulating) and of imagining a grand metaphysical scheme in which sun and moon, male and female images, seasonal patterns, and the uses of elements and colors all play a part. They evoke a response from all readers, even those most remote from the day and the place of creation. To keep that balance means that we do not separate art from life, symbols from the biological basis of culture. We all know that poetry is bio-basic. Painting is another example of the way in which the artist vitalizes our surroundings. Impressionists conjured up values of repose by catching the instant, and their hedonistic awareness of the outdoors became literally consumable by sensuous amateurs at home. In contrast, the symbolic values of cubism seemed to privilege the intellect over the body, and tended toward a negation of the fleeting moment by the addition of the time dimension to their pictures. While the imagery favored by Cubists was artificial, man-made, the Impressionists luxuriated in the natural. All were responding, although in such strikingly different manners, to man's basic concern with time, with his own mortality. But this thought did not occur to me in the first essay I wrote, a comparison of Stevens with the French painters he liked so much. It had to wait until I was able to formulate a plan of Stevens' psychological evolution with the help of Gilbert Durand's major treatise, *Les Structures anthropologiques de l'imaginaire* (Paris, 1961). It was a systematization of Gaston Bachelard's studies of the material imagination (the four elements) which later Bachelard himself had redistributed along two main axes: ascensional-descensional and inner-outer. Starting from Bergson's famous definition, in *The Two Sources of Morality and Religion*, which held the imagination to be a defense of the body against the inevitability of death perceived by the intelligence of man, Durand answered for me the questions I had asked myself, in the essays, about the comparability of Stevens with other poets and painters. His anthropological approach was in agreement with Stevens' idea of man, with my need for a small set of symbolic values on which to base comparisons.

According to Gilbert Durand there are three basic schemes, or anthropological itineraries, which enable man to cope with vital fears. He can *sublimate* death by an angel's flight (or, in reverse, a monster's fright); he can *euphemize* it by dreams of descent into the hollows of a maternal shelter; he can *master* it by myths of eternal return or cyclic progress. To a phenomenology of the imagination which distinguishes images that go up and out, down and into, and round and round, Durand added a problematic reflexology (up means erect posture, down means digestion, round means copulation), and plugged in the Jungian archetypology (especially the Hero, the Mother, and the androgynous Godhead). He also showed the relationship between these symbols and the tripartite division of primitive society into warrior, peasant, and priest-king, particularly as they developed into Indo-European archaeology (Dumézil). Further expansion of his system could encompass personality psychology with specific reference to Erich Neumann's *Origins of Consciousness* and its phases of primordial oneness with the mother, individuation (the heroic fight), and centroversion (conciliation of opposites). Neumann is perhaps even more useful than Durand in helping us to understand how major shifts in imagery occur, how it is possible for a poet to find affinities with widely diverging works of imagination at different times along his evolution. Durand can be adapted all the more easily to the work of the Symbolists, as they are poets whose primary interest in the spirals of their own imagination confirms his groupings. When Stevens observes "an up and down between sun and moon" (*C.P.* 34) in his early poetry, or later on that the hero is he who "of repetition is most master" (*C.P.* 406) he invites us to examine the metaphorical placer of these nuggets of self-knowledge. Suddenly a larger pattern disengages itself. The links between unconscious psychological values and forms of expression, between psychological shifts and historical events, become visible in the light of comparisons. What independently of this research had appeared in Roy Pearce's *Continuity of American Poetry* (Princeton, 1961) as the successive modes of Stevens' development can be reinterpreted as *structures* corresponding to the profound transformations of his symbols, symptoms themselves of deep psychological changes. As a preliminary survey of my claims, here are a few stakes:

1. What Roy Pearce called the "descriptive and dramatic mode" in *Harmonium* evolved from symbols of intimacy, hedonistic joy, and incarnation preceding the 1923-1924 balance between lunar and solar symbols, between hedonistic and heroic values. Actually it is the poetry that predated *Harmonium*, the earlier poetry unpublished by Stevens, which seems more characteristic of a mood very close to Keats's empathy and to Baudelaire's *correspondances*. The logic of this poetry is analogy and similitude, its verbal schema includes descending, concealing, merging. Its archetypal epithets are "green," "warm," "concealed," "inside." Its archetypal nouns symbolize night, dwelling, color, food, vegetation, connoting the presence of the Mother, while its tombs, boats, islands, and disguises convey the image of death partly hidden and beautified as Moon.

2. The "abstracting process," which begins a little before *Ideas of Order* but fully develops in *The Man with the Blue Guitar* and *Parts of a World*, links the birth of Stevens' hero with an antithetic and expository style closer to Cubism than to Symbolism. Its geometries and schizoïd structures suggest idealization and a recoil from sensual reality, and its verbs of separation, its adjectives of purity ("blue," "pure," "naked") suggest a hero's fight against "indulgences." This is the Stevens of the process of individuation, age fifty, angel versus feminine monster of the unconscious, mountain-top versus depth, eagle against spider. The sun, light, and air, Nietzsche's Alps, are the poet's friends. (Until I completed

the last essay in this collection, these two structures monopolized my attention: the reader will see how they alternated in the Impressionist-Cubist impulses I described in the Stevens and painting essay; how the heroism discounted the Laforgue analogy; how Baudelaire and Mallarmé also seemed to fit on either side of this cleavage between *Harmonium* and the middle period from 1930 to 1940; how, finally, the evolution of Stevens from Impressionism to Cubism repeated itself, for psychological as well as historical reasons, in Apollinaire's two periods. Until I wrote the fifth essay I put off a comparison based on the possibility of a conciliation, a marriage of the sun and moon—that is to say, a third structure born of the conflicting elements.)

3. To what Pearce justly named the "dialectical mode" of *Transport to Summer* correspond the great epiphanies of Stevens' controversion. His logic shifts from "contrary theses" to the conciliation of opposites. His rhetoric of repetition, circular sentences, metaphorical and stanzaic circles espouses the cycle of seasons and celebrates the marriage of the Self's two halves.

4. *The Rock* (1955) stands apart as symbol of desymbolization or "decreation." The end of the imagination (itself imagined) has been reached by a jump outside time, outside death, at least in a handful of poems.

These groupings may be too sharp. Because great poets tend to imitate themselves throughout their poetry a sense of thematic oneness blurs the phases of Stevens' development. But taken as models of those elements in Stevens' poetry which did change, these structures account for his affinities with French poets (Baudelaire, Mallarmé) as well as his evolution, especially in his third phase, away from anything resembling Symbolism. In my second attempt at relations between Stevens and painting ("Apollinaire and Cubism") the structural models helped me to situate Picasso's guitar at the heroic moment of Stevens' second phase. His blind spot about Surrealism did not prevent him from seeking the same state of spiritual wholeness as those latter-day alchemists. That quest, mainly in his third and fourth phases, is the subject of my last essay.

If I may shift the perspective to my own debts, intellectual and otherwise, I take pleasure in naming my benefactors: Samuel French Morse, who opened all the doors for my research when I first arrived in this country to work on Stevens in 1956, and Roy Harvey Pearce, who has encouraged me by his published example, by his direct influence, by his solicitude as colleague, friend, and mentor. For her gentle insistence and sustained confidence in spite of my long intermittences I also wish to express my gratitude to Miriam Brokaw, Associate Director of Princeton Press, who fears neither space nor time in the service of scholarship.

La Jolla, November 1970

1

Poetry and Painting

The arrangement conceals the desire of
The artist. But one confides in what has no
Concealed creator. One walks easily

The unpainted shore, accepts the world
As anything but sculpture. Good-bye,
Mrs. Pappadopoulos, and thanks.

("So and So Reclining on a Couch")

WHETHER the influence of painting on poetry is desirable is an old question and possibly an otiose one. With the advent of impressionism and succeeding schools, the poetic principles underlying art have become more visible; less "word painting" (in the awkward sense of much eighteenth-century description and Parnassian verse for art's sake) has been taking place, and more sharing in the imaginative metamorphosis wrought upon nature by the painter's brush. Many modern poets, in whose ranks I muster at random Baudelaire, Mallarmé, Rilke, Apollinaire, John Peale Bishop, and Wallace Stevens, have acknowledged their debt to painters or sculptors and their poetry has grown the richer by that debt. The point no longer is whether the critics should compare poetry and painting, but how they can do so without being "laocoönized."

This risk may be taken the more cheerfully since Stevens himself showed the way in his critical writing. He was—like Valéry, another poet with a painter's eye and a refined mental museum—extremely conscious of the processes of creation. We can avail ourselves of a paper entitled "The Relations Between Poetry and Painting," which Stevens read at the Museum of Modern Art in 1951, and in which he defined four main areas of influence: sensibility, subject matter, technique, and aesthetics. He did not cite his own work as illustration, but he was so careful to keep to the craftsman's viewpoint, discarding any mysterious *Zeitgeist*, that his words bear the sigil of self-analysis. He said, in effect, that a poet can learn his trade by reading what painters reveal about theirs, and by looking at their pictures. It is not irrelevant that Stevens was a great reader of exhibition cata-

WALLACE STEVENS
and the Symbolist Imagination

logues. He called them "the natural habitat for prose poems"[1] and wrote notes for catalogues in praise of Dufy, Grommaire, and the obscure Jean Labasque. He took equal heed of studio oracles and the doctrines of Croce, Berenson, and Focillon. Not only his lectures but his poems abound in references to Cézanne, Picasso, and many others. He was probably among the first in America to see Cubist paintings, thanks to his Harvard acquaintance Walter C. Arensberg, who knew Duchamp and Gleizes, and whose studio on West Seventh Street was a favorite haunt of the Kreymborg sodality.[2] Stevens' own eclectic collection of French paintings ("I have a taste for Braque and a purse for Bombois," he once complained in a letter to his Paris art dealer) displayed his attraction to Impressionism and Cubism. But his poems tell even more about his dependence on art than his lectures and pictures do.

One feels in the poetic universe of Wallace Stevens a sort of pulse that alternately dilates and narrows the field of vision. At its widest it resembles the world of an open-air landscapist; at the other extreme, it has the limits of a painter's studio. One pole corresponds to the broad landscapes of the Impressionists, its opposite to the still lifes and the compositions of decorative Cubism.

The more lasting influence on Stevens' vision was perhaps that of Impressionism, which he called "the only great thing in modern art." He regarded it as "poetic."[3] By this, it

[1] *O.P.*, p. 290.
[2] See Alfred Kreymborg, *Troubadour*, New York, 1957, p. 220.
[3] "Notes on Jean Labasque," *O.P.*, p. 293.

seems to me that he meant an element of sensibility, a sensitiveness to the flux and change of nature. Both Monet and Stevens express the poetry of a fluent universe, a vast stage for the wind, rain, sun, and moonlight, a poem of skies and waters in which the key word is weather. Their insistence on weather, season of year, and time of day stems from an acute sense of visible changes caused by the condition of lighting. The great Impressionists, Monet, Sisley, and Pissarro, carried this concern to the extreme that they no longer painted objects so much as the light on them and the air round them. Stevens, who dubbed himself "pundit of the weather," wrote "Evening Without Angels" as a hymn to "the great interests of man: air and light." Blue shadows, "Blue Building in the Summer Air," a gold tree which is blue—air is everywhere. And a chameleon light plays in dozens of poems with suggestive titles: "Variations on a Summer Day," "Of Hartford in a Purple Light," and, most magnificent of all, "Sea Surface Full of Clouds." Presumably the poet never saw the series of the "Water Lilies" in the Orangerie Museum, for he never went to Paris. Yet all the feeling of the old painter of Giverny for the fleeting reflections of light in iridescent water inspires this picture of the ocean:

> The sea-clouds whitened far below the calm
> And moved, as blooms move, in the swimming green
> And in the watery radiance, while the hue
>
> Of heaven in an antique reflection rolled
> Round those flotillas. And sometimes the sea
> Poured brilliant iris on the glistening blue.

WALLACE STEVENS
and the Symbolist Imagination

The fascination of this spectacle results in a fusion of the consciousness with the external world. It is hard to say whether the five different aspects of the sea bring about the succeeding moods of the poem, or the reverse. Visual appearance and mental reality are one.

Stevens' saying in "Men by the Thousand" that "the soul is composed of the external world" gives a clue to what happens in "Sea Surface Full of Clouds," "The Snow Man," and countless other poems in which the mind of the beholder mirrors his surroundings and fluctuates with the slightest change of light. This impressionistic theory of environment culminates in the fourth section of "The Comedian as the Letter C," with its anti-intellectual statement that "His soil is Man's intelligence," an extreme, although not unnatural, consequence of Stevens' delight in the sheen and bloom "of the surface of things."

A constant preoccupation of the Impressionist, whether painter or poet, is to restore the innocence of the eye. Monet wished he were temporarily blind, to experience sight again and see the world anew. Similarly, Wallace Stevens yearned to be the giant on Mount Chocorua, whose sensibility strikes us as thoroughly impressionistic:

> The feeling of him was the feel of day,
> And of a day as yet unseen, in which
> To see was like to be.[4]

His impulse toward transparence, his desire to be "at the center of a diamond," his obsession with the freshness, or,

---

[4] "Chocorua to Its Neighbor." Unless otherwise stated all poems can be found in *C.P.*

in his own refreshing phrase, the fraîcheur of sight, bespeak the impressionist's dream of a translucent vision, free from memory and artifice. He wrote, in a letter to his Paris art dealer: "I share your pleasure in the Impressionistic school. In the pictures of this school: so light in tone, so bright in color, one is not conscious of the medium. The pictures are like nature. . . ."[5]

But very often what he saw was "Nature as pinakothek" and what he felt was "weather by Franz Hals." The freshness of Stevens' poetry is largely due to what Delmore Schwartz called "a vision instructed in the museums," rather than to the glass-pane purity of naked sight. Was not the very transparence which he praised in impressionistic landscapes a product of artifice? The posthumously published "Anecdote of the Abnormal" gives a revealing documentation of Stevens' attitude:

> The common grass is green.
> But there are regions where the grass
> Assumes a pale Italianate sheen—
> Is almost Byzantine.
> . . . new colors make new things
> And new things make old things again.[6]

This voluptuary of the eye needed an ever-renewed flow of novel sensations. Art was his remedy against "the malady" of the quotidian; its colors dispelled the slate color of habit, were a vital part of his poetic diet. He may very well go on record as a naturalist who thrived on artificiality.

[5] Letter to Mlle Paule Vidal, 30 January 1948, *L.W.S.*, p. 577.
[6] *O.P.*, pp. 23-24.

WALLACE STEVENS
and the Symbolist Imagination

Parts of a World and later collections, too, seem cluttered with the paraphernalia of Cubism, the guitars and mandolins, the still lifes arranged on tables, the plaster heads, the bits and odds that painters hoard for their collages, parts of a world rescued from the dump. To the reader looking for Stevens' subject, it may appear that the use of art as a source of inspiration entails a narrowing of the poetic range, limited as it is to studio objects. There is some truth in this opinion, and much superficiality. Certainly, the absence of man as a pictorial theme seems to me as conspicuous in Stevens' poems as in modern painting since Monet, excepting Picasso's Ingrist period. No nudes in the traditional sense, only grotesque caricatures. The human shape has lost its supremacy and its dignity. For an analysis of this fact, we have only to look at Projection A of "So-and-So Reclining on a Couch," a mere mechanism of curves and color, "completely anonymous." In like fashion, the figure in the first stanza of "Sunday Morning" has not the slightest, even suggested, feature; as in a picture by Matisse, it is sacrificed to a decorative pattern.

But the real subject of Stevens' poetry and the real subject of Cubist painting is not immediately perceptible: it is poetic imagination. The merit of the poem or picture arises from the degree of concentration with which the imagination refracts the object. The meanest and most derelict thing can thus be made significant, beautiful. "A Post-Card from the Volcano" typifies this procedure; it shows

> A dirty house in a gutted world,
> A tatter of shadows peaked to white,
> Smeared with the gold of the opulent sun.

—a gold that performs the same imaginative function as the chrome yellow enhancing the dried-up fishes painted by Georges Braque. Stevens teaches us that the center of modern art is metamorphosis.

"To increase the aspects of experience" sometimes demands an artifice of perception. The multiple perspective of the cubist, the dance round the object which causes Picasso to add an eye to his profiles, or the shifting optics of Cézanne, by virtue of which a saucer seems to bulge on either side of a bottle placed in front of it—these modes of vision stress the role of an imaginative eye exploring the hidden facets of an object. This method can also serve in poetry, as evidenced by "Thirteen Ways of Looking at a Blackbird" or, in a more pictorial vein, the twelve views of a pineapple encompassed in "Someone Puts a Pineapple together."[7] The latter poem documents Picasso's saying, twice cited by Stevens, that a picture is a hoard of destructions.[8] Originally this phrase described the procedure of analytical Cubism, exploding the object into prismatic fragments. The effect was one of complexity; the picture became a simultaneous enumeration of related aspects. Stevens' pineapple is treated in much the same way. It is the "sum of its complications." By this, the poet means that the total reality of the fruit will be recomposed from the twelve pieces which make up its epistemological profile: a hut and palms,

[7] N.A., pp. 83-87.
[8] In "The Man with the Blue Guitar," Sec. xv, it reads "hoard of destructions"; in "The Relations Between Poetry and Painting," it is "horde." The first spelling appears again in Renato Poggioli's translation, with Stevens' comment that he found the saying in Christian Zervos' book on Picasso.

an owl covered with eyes, nailed-up lattices, etc. Nine of the twelve resemblances are visual. The complete poem adds up to a performance as witty as any Picasso *circa* 1910.

Why write a poem about a pineapple, this "incredible subject for poetry"? Stevens chose it for the same reason as the Cubist chose his studio arrangement, because it was

> A wholly artificial nature in which
> The profusion of metaphor has been increased.
> . . . fertile in more than changes of light
> On the table or in the color of the room.

This comes in defense of artificiality. Some privileged objects, however meaningless to the unpoetic, have such a shape as lends itself to metamorphosis: palms, fans, the open hand, certain fruit and flowers, a blackbird, and the sinuous guitar, friendly to the Cubist's dreams. But some other things resist imagination, defeat the poet's will. Among them certain roses in sunlight, "too much as they are to be changed by metaphor,"[9] and two obdurate pears that will "resemble nothing else."[10] Sister Bernetta Quinn rightly called our attention to this "victory of the real over the fictive."[11] Only when nature imitates art is it favorable to pictorial transmutation.

Thus the poetry of Wallace Stevens incorporates conflicting elements from Impressionism and Cubism: naturalness and artificiality, delight in appearances and metamorphosis of appearances. A baffling sum of relations—for

[9] "Bouquet of roses in Sunlight."
[10] "Study of Two Pears."
[11] Sister Bernetta M. Quinn, "Metamorphosis in Wallace Stevens," *Sewanee Review*, Spring, 1952.

where in these extreme ranges is the identity of a poet's sensibility?

The identity is in Stevens' concern with change. Impressionism shows the *passive* principle of change. The eye must be as candid as possible and merely relay the variations of light and colors. But in Cubism, "more than changes of light" are involved. Imagination is the *active* principle which transforms and extends the object by multiplying resemblances. The metaphors of poetry and the metamorphoses of painting tap the same reservoir of analogies.

At first glance any attempt to compare the form of a poem and that of a picture seems either futile or faulty. The ghosts of Lessing and Irving Babbitt loom before us voicing fearful interdictions. Yet, if we are to heed Stevens' hint about relating his poetic technique to painting, we must cross the old barrier between arts of space and arts of time and the new one between discursive and presentational forms.[12]

What is meant by form? A poem with its sequence of vowels and consonants offers a temporal medium entirely alien to the spatial medium of a picture: lines, tone value, and colors. The otherness, the radical heterogeneity of these pure, basic, *primary* forms cannot be overemphasized. At their level, beauty seems divorced from what is generally understood by meaning—it has only formal significance. But a poem and a picture have a *secondary* form which is intimately fused with their meaning. It is in this sense of the word form that the composition of an ode by Keats

---

[12] Cf. in John Peale Bishop's *Collected Essays*, New York, 1948, "Poetry and Paintings," an essay showing the time element in pictures and the spatial element in poems.

WALLACE STEVENS
and the Symbolist Imagination

may strike Allen Tate as pictorial, that Marcel Proust wrote about the metaphors in Elstir's seascapes, that Wallace Stevens may speak of the diction of a portrait by Giorgione. So long as they do not involve primary forms, such comparisons are enlightening and legitimately drawn. The structure, imagery, and diction of Stevens' poems afford many relations of this kind with the devices and effects of painting.

The best example of Stevens' pictorial method of composition is to be found in the structure of "Sunday Morning," his most celebrated long poem. Its form is a meditative monologue, now in the first, now in the third person. Superficially the poem is tied together by references to the central character: she dreams, she says, etc. But is it really a discursive presentation of arguments with dialectic progression? It must have seemed so in the form of its first appearance in the November 1915 issue of *Poetry*. There, the poem had five stanzas, and this five-stanza version has had fairly wide currency ever since. But the truth is that Stevens originally wrote "Sunday Morning" in the eight-stanza version which was to appear in the first edition of *Harmonium* in 1923. It was Miss Harriet Monroe who persuaded Stevens to publish the five-stanza version. In assenting to this disfigurement of his work, the poet tried to make the best of an editorial botch by putting immediately after stanza one the final stanza of his original version. But this alteration made the poem look like a discursive argument, with the first four stanzas referring to the central character and the fifth as a possible answer to her questions.

The poem as we have it in *Harmonium* erases the discursive quality and restores the original design. The central character loses her prominence; the narrative fabric is disrupted. The full-length version is the better poem. It has more unity, which results from its pictorial composition. "Sunday Morning" is not a succession of ideas, but of pictures. Stanza one is organized as a dyptich—on one panel, a woman in a chair, oranges, a cockatoo, a rich, Matisse-like arrangement on an Oriental rug; on the other side, a sombre lake; silence accentuates the pictorial quality. The sense of space is enhanced by the simile "as a calm darkens," protracted by "the day is like wide water." This antithetic pattern, a picture of earthly life alternating with a scene of another world, continues in the next six stanzas. A complete resolution of the form occurs in the last stanza, for it corresponds panel for panel to the first dyptich, but in reverse order. This formal chiasmic symmetry heightens our aesthetic enjoyment. The poem is framed between two visions of earth; its formal beauty depends partly on the vividness of these visions, partly on the perfect balance of its structure.

The effect of the pictorial method of composition is a tension within a balance. The atmosphere of "Sunday Morning" is anything but tense. Stevens was not in that sense a dramatic poet. There is no tenseness, but a tension —not dramatic, but spatial. Its springs from the juxtaposition of antithetic blocks. The pattern of the sequence shows that the poem winds up as a complete circle. The *Poetry* version did not. And yet the final version of "Sunday Morning" has more force, perhaps a centripetal force. It achieves emotional impact within the visual daydreaming of an inconclusive meditation. It represents the triumph of a nondramatic poet over his own limitations.

WALLACE STEVENS
and the Symbolist Imagination

The preceding remark by no means sets a claim that Stevens always composed pictorially. But, granting that his best poems are those with dramatic force, it may be that this dramatic force is best supported and actualized by their pictorial structure. A piece like "Mrs. Alfred Uruguay" does not draw its force from the rhetorical violence of its beginning ("So what said the others and the sun went down"), but rather from the spatial opposition of the two symbolic central figures. We are dealing with a poet gifted with a strong visual imagination, who presents conflicts of ideas as conflicts of forms and shapes.

Such a method of composition supposes the ability to create pictorial images, that is, representations of visual elements of reality organized pictorially. In Stevens' imagery, refined by Imagist experimentation and observations of artistic devices, we thrill at the wealth of sensuous perceptions of shapes, lights, and colors. Yet we are never allowed to forget the symbolic meaning of each pictorial effect. Stevens was not, like Gautier, a painter *manqué*.

In "The Idea of Order at Key West," we are offered both the theory and the practice of "the maker's rage to order the words of the sea." This is a poem about poetic creation and, by way of illustration, the poet evokes an image of a port at nightfall. The order of the description suggests the brush of a painter organizing his pictorial space. The perspective he defines with sure repetitions becomes a symbol of the victory of art over chaos. The verbs carry the magic of his art: mastering, deepening, enchanting; the nouns and adjectives are fraught with pictorial vividness: fiery poles, glassy lights, emblazoned zones.

If perspective symbolizes poetry, flatness connotes the unpoetic. Let us look at the pen-and-ink drawing entitled "The Common Life":

> That's the down-town frieze,
> Principally the church steeple,
> A black line beside a white line;
> And the stack of the electric plant,
> A black line drawn on flat air.
>
> .   .   .   .   .   .
>
> The paper is whiter
> For these black lines.
>
> .   .   .   .   .   .
>
> The paper is whiter.
> The men have no shadows
> And the women have only one side.

The whole poem is a single image, in which the vocabulary achieves the economy of Klee's calligraphic technique. But again symbolism gives poetic meaning to plastic effects. The straight lines, the glaring contrast of black and white, the absence of depth and shadows, are metaphors for the spiritual vacuity of modern life. "Sad Strains of a Gay Waltz" and "Poem with Rhythms" afford two additional examples of this plastic symbolism, which equates shadowlessness to imaginative poverty and shadows to the life of the imagination.

Light imagery is vital to Stevens. Light is motion, change, and cheerfulness. For its evanescent appearances the poet has developed a special "vernacular of light," of which he gives us a glimpse in "Variations of a Summer Day":

WALLACE STEVENS
and the Symbolist Imagination

> Words for the dazzle
> Of mica, the dithering of glass,
> The Arachne integument of dead trees
> Are the eye grown larger, more intense.

Just as a painter will seek the challenge of light flashing on shiny objects, Stevens is lured by the glitter of crystals, diamonds, pieces of "broken glass in the grass." He seeks hard bright surfaces like bronze, tinsel, mirrors, ice, in which color is toughened by a sense of touch, a process of synaesthesia defined in the nutshell of this image: "emerald becoming emeralds."

The sharp outline and the bright surface of the forms result from the quality of light in which things are seen—a cold light for the most part, "more like snowy air," "an acid light" etching the contours of things, sharpening them with shadows. These are the "lights masculine" at work in "Of Hartford in a Purple Light," sculpturing shapes of the river, the railroad, the cathedral. But there are also "lights feminine," in which "every muscle slops away." Fewer poems belong to this late-Impressionistic type of imagery than to the masculine, clear-cut group. They are mostly about, or rather of, night; glitterings are toned down to glistenings, shapes merge into shades. Night is a female, soft as a woman's arm, bathed in the formlessness of green which permeates and fuses everything.[13] In those images, we truly sense "a painter's light."[14] It comes to life; entering the spatial milieu

[13] "Six Significant Landscapes," stanza 2; "Phosphor Reading by his own Light."

[14] "The Poet Who Lived with His Words," a poem by Samuel French Morse, *The Tuftonian*, XIII (Winter 1957).

created by words, called on stage by metaphors, it acts like "women whispering" or like a lion with "ruddy claws" and "frothy jaws," actualizing in poetry Focillon's notion that light can become a form in itself.[15]

Stevens' gifts as a colorist shine particularly in his color matches. His palette glitters with the cheerfulness of the Impressionists. Its light tones are gaudy, with the etymological meaning of gay, never garish, for complementary associations are carefully avoided in favor of more fastidious marriages. But even images that seem purely pictorial call our attention from the poet's descriptive skill to his chromatic symbolism and his exhilarating sense of language. Let me quote two Imagist tours de force from *Harmonium*:

> Last night we sat beside a pool of pink
> Clippered with lilies scudding the bright chromes.[16]

The color contrast is heightened by a clash between the subdued alliteration of plosives in the first line and the consonance of harsh "k" sounds in the second line. But the pleasure derived from this feat of virtuosity would seem a little cheap were it not for the startling nautical metaphor with its ironical overtones attuned to the context. Likewise, a typical image from "The Comedian as the Letter C" creates an acute contrast between color areas:

> The green palmettoes in crepuscular ice
> Clipped frigidly blue black meridians,
> Morose chiaroscuro, gauntly drawn.

[15] "The Glass of Water" and H. Focillon, *La Vie des formes dans l'art*, Paris, 1964, p. 37.
[16] "Le Monocle de Mon Oncle," stanza xi.

WALLACE STEVENS
and the Symbolist Imagination

Just enough studio jargon for the sake of strangeness and to give a feeling for the degree of heat which painters consider important in the arrangement of colors. But the psychological effect of the picture, its morose, gaunt, icy, crepuscular mood, extends much further than the merely visual impression. Stevens was never content with "verbal painting," if such a thing exists in poetry. He said in one of his *Adagia*: "Poetry as an imaginative thing consists of more than lies on the surface."[17] Poetry lies when it tries to compete with painting. Color is in painting the real thing, in poetry a reflection of words. The true nature of an image is to become a metaphor.

Stevens' color symbolism is mostly a personal affair, based as it is on a lifelong meditation of the subjective quality of all perceptions. It starts with "Three Travellers Watch a Sunrise," and ends with "Two Illustrations that the World is what you Make of It." We shall explore only its relations with painting.

One element in the "broken color" of the Impressionist is that the eye transforms two colors into a single tone. Stevens used the device repeatedly. A lemon is "yellow-blue, yellow-green." The lilac in "Arcades of Philadelphia the Past" shows in the eye of the beholder,

> . . . in the agate eye, red blue
> Red purple, never quite red itself.

Pure, essential red is never seen, because it is abstract. In "Woman Looking at a Vase of Flowers" pure red is called

[17] *O.P.*, p. 161.

"inhuman," and in "The Bouquet" the distinction between the particular of the eye and the abstract of the imagination clarifies the whole matter. The colors of things "are questions of the looks they get," but these colors, "seen in insight," become symbols. So the blue of the sky comes to mean the blue of the imagination. But it never ceases to denote the sky, because, essentially like a painter, Stevens always elaborates from sense data. Even when color tends toward abstraction, he never allows it to lose its sensuous quality. His last collection of verse, *The Rock*, restates an artist's love of color in this exultant flow of images:

> And a blue broke on him from the sun,
> A bullioned blue, a blue abulge,
>
> Like daylight, with time's bellishings,
> And sensuous summer stood full-height.

Such richly metaphorical visions play the same role in our enjoyment of poetry as the sensuous pulsing of color in Van Gogh's landscapes. But only the artistry of poetic language can stimulate in the reader these chromatic impressions. "Domination of Black," which Stevens at one time called his favorite poem in *Harmonium*, has no pictorial source. The only word denoting a specific color is in the title. Yet the poem releases a fantasia of colors that has the musicality of an abstract picture by Manessier or Bazaine.

Stevens' use of pictorial imagery, his plastic and chromatic symbolism, his art of composition, reveal how closely his poetry can approximate the effects of painting without lapsing into what Louis Untermeyer mistook for "verbal mosaics in which syllables are used as pigment."[18] We know now that there is as much symbolism and sense for "the edges of language" in *Harmonium* as in later works. However, the proportion of Imagistic experiments in color diminishes from *Harmonium* to *The Rock*, as belonging to a style which Stevens took for granted, and also because the emphasis shifts gradually from style to feeling and thought, from description of the world to the "world as meditation." If the reader expects in the valedictory poems the kind of pictorial technique he enjoyed in the liminary pieces, he is likely to be disappointed. After *Harmonium*, we have, significantly, *Ideas of Order*; after the practice, the theory. But then Stevens, even when he theorizes on aesthetics, always remains a poet. For him the imagination identified itself with something big, blue, glittering, and sharply outlined. His ideas on poetry had a visual, sensory, rather than an abstract origin.

One unmistakable sign of Stevens' indebtedness to the aesthetics of modern painting is the frequency with which the words "perception," "object," and "reality" recur in his poems. Another clue inscribed in his critical vocabulary is the use of the verb "to paint" meaning to create, and the noun "paint" for poetry. A quantity of poems illustrate the profoundest problems of artistic creation in terms of painting. Beyond mere verbal features, this alliance fostered a symbolism of shapes standing for aesthetic notions. There were two realities for Stevens—the reality of things observed and the reality of things imagined. One, the world, was in

[18] Louis Untermeyer, *Modern American Poetry*, New York, 1925, p. 326.

the image of a beast, a lion, a monster; the other, the poem, was an angel, "the necessary angel" of reality. Perception places the artist in contact with reality, with the beast. Sometimes, as we have seen, nature resists the imagination. Then a conflict arises between the object and the will, "a war that never ends" between the imagination and the monster of nature. When Stevens comes to grips with the monster, his "rage for order" resembles Cézanne's. In a sense, his aesthetics were Cézanne's subjective ("expressing oneself") objectivism ("realizing the object"). It is a personal meeting, an encounter with reality on terms of equality. This at least echoes the wish of "The Man with a Blue Guitar":

> That I may reduce the monster to
> Myself, and then may be myself
>
> In face of the monster, be more than part
> Of it, more than the monstrous player of
>
> One of its monstrous lutes. . . .

And when he gives full attention to the object, the poet defines poetry, in the very words of Cézanne's roughhewn aesthetics, as

> An exercise in viewing the world.
> On the motive![19]

Cézanne is the tribal god of modern painting because, as Stevens saw it, he has "helped to create a new reality, a modern reality . . . , a reality of decreation."[20] Rilke remarks that Cézanne's apples have become "indestructible in their

[19] "Variations on a Summer Day."
[20] N.A., p. 174.

obstinate existence."[21] They are different from edible fruit, though not less real. Their reality is poetic. They have been decreated and the painter has given them being. In modern art, at least among the votaries of Cézanne, essence is no longer divine, it is poetic,

> The essential poem at the center of things.[22]

Cézanne had only one word: to realize. By this he meant very much the same thing as Stevens in his declaration of "An Ordinary Evening in New Haven":

> We seek

> The poem of pure reality, untouched
> By trope or deviation, straight to the word,
> Straight to the transfixing object, to the object

> At the exactest point at which it is itself,
> Transfixing by being purely what it is,
> A view of New Haven, say, through the certain eye,

> The eye made clear of uncertainty, with the sight
> Of simple seeing, without reflection. We seek
> Nothing beyond reality.

This pure reality is the monster mastered and purified by imagination.

From the encounter with the monster to the fusion with the angel of pure reality, Stevens' aesthetics has gone a long way. It bridges the gap between a painting of sheer appearances and an art which creates its own reality "in face of the monster." It reconciles the Impressionist vision and Cézanne's world within a world.

[21] *Letters*, New York, 1945, I, p. 304.   [22] "A Primitive Like an Orb."

A final point remains for discussion. Even granting the enrichment of the poetic sensibility inspired by painting and the virtuosity of Stevens' transpositions from pictures, always under the deft control of poetic form, even granting this positive gain, there is a great danger that our approach may have done injustice to Stevens in the reader's mind. Through his affinities with other art lovers such as Proust, he might end up in the pigeonhole of aestheticism. Art buffers the aesthete from harsh realities. A vision of the world mediated by art is of the second degree—or even, in a Platonic perspective, of the third. But surely this cannot be the whole story about Stevens, in whom "the native element,"[23] the sense of the importance of living in an external world, counterbalanced the impulse to neutralize nature and hold it at arm's length like a picture. And the impulse to grapple with the "monster" is the aesthetic equivalent of Stevens' respect for external reality. All we can presume to do is to take stock of the art-nature duality in Stevens.

The question of why Stevens and many other poets have been so dependent on the arts for their vision of the world has metaphysical implications. Pascal was critical of the reality of painting because he believed in a transcendental truth that dwarfed art to the status of all other human delusions. But we live in an age of disbelief. What makes Stevens a modern poet, i.e., a poet of our time, is this modern consciousness that the arts compensate for our lost belief. Stevens was no solemn worshipper of painting and he had often enough a self-mocking word for the amateurs at Du-

[23] Samuel F. Morse, "The Native Element, *Kenyon Review*, xx (Summer 1958), 446-465.

rand-Ruel's. But his practice of poetry echoes the intent faith of Baudelaire in the divine testimony of art, or rather, to avoid the term faith, Malraux's creed that art is "la monnaie de l'absolu," the currency, but also the small change of the absolute. Understood as the poetic and moral principle of an order protecting us from chaos, art becomes more than a source of beautiful shapes and colors; it becomes a "supreme fiction," an inspiration tentatively analogous to the idea of god,

> For a moment final, in the way
> The thinking of art seems final when
>
> The idea of god is smoky dew.[24]

[1957, 1959]

[24] "The Man with the Blue Guitar," stanza VI.

2

Jules Laforgue

. . . under every no
Lay a passion for yes that had never been broken.

("*Esthétique du Mal*")

T. S. ELIOT, in acknowledging his debt to Laforgue,[1] re-
marked that the smaller poet is more likely than the great
master to influence a young writer. This may account for
Laforgue's sway over dozens of poets from Pound to Crane.
It also suggests that tricks of technique and mannerisms of
form are more readily transferable than great themes and
deep thoughts, at least to the fledgling awed by the big
names of literature. Part of Laforgue's present renown is the
afterglow of the reputation earned by poets who went to him
as obscure young men. It cannot be dissociated from the
achievements of these poets, among whom the greatest are
Americans, any more than they can be understood apart
from him.

Wallace Stevens never so much as mentioned Laforgue in
print. However a legend, now threadbare, clothes him in the
garb of Pierrot. Paul Rosenfeld started it, and René Taupin
gave it wide currency. Warren Ramsey wisely left Stevens
out of his book on the Laforguian ironic heritage, but on
second thought wrote a few comments in an article about
"Wallace Stevens and some French Poets."[2] But the first
serious treatment of Laforgue's influence on *Harmonium* was
H. R. Hays's study, written twenty years earlier.[3] Hays's par-
ticular merit was to call attention to the differences between
Stevens' and Laforgue's sensibilities and to a few technical
borrowings. But he was too prompt in prophesying that
Harmonium, first published in 1923, would not be followed
by any work indicating a change in Stevens' viewpoint. With

[1] "Talk on Dante," *The Adelphi*, (January-March 1951), 106-07.
[2] *Trinity Review*, VIII (May 1954), 36-40.
[3] "Laforgue and Stevens," *RR*, XXV (1934), 242-48.

WALLACE STEVENS
and the Symbolist Imagination

the perspective afforded by the publication of *The Collected Poems* in 1954 and the *Opus Posthumous* in 1957, it is now possible to take a long view of Laforgue's influence on him. The divergences of theme and thought become sharper, the parallelisms of technique more visible. It was the artist in Laforgue, and not the Pierrot, who attracted Stevens most. It is less the irony than the Impressionism that seems a common feature of both poets' sensibilities. Art, then, was the mediator of their timeless appointment together.

Both Laforgue and Stevens may be termed poets without a subject, at least as the usual expectation of "subject" goes. But if we are merely looking for a central concern uniting their poems, the single subject of Laforgue, his own ego, becomes quite obvious and distinct from Stevens' quest of a poetic Self defeating the ego. Hopping from the Earth to the Moon and from the Unconscious to Pierrot's stage, Laforgue tried to eschew the demands of egocentrism, but he would always come back to his baffling, tender, hypochondriac self:

> Mon cœur est trop, ah trop central![4]

The heart image is the most recurrent one in even as unself-centered a work as *Le Sanglot de la terre*. The astronomical popularizations of Flammarion, which Warren Ramsey convincingly suggests as the background to that book, must have left Laforgue as frightened as was Pascal by the discoveries of Copernicus.[5] The "I" of Laforgue, like Pascal's, lurks in

[4] "Dimanches," *Des Fleurs de bonne volonté, Œuvres complètes de Jules Laforgue*, Paris, 1951, II, 31.

[5] Compare "Dans le silence noir du calme sans écho" ("Marche Funèbre") with Pascal's "Le Silence éternel de ces espaces infinis. . . ."

the darkness of his cosmic pessimism. But in *Les Complaintes* it comes out in the open:

> Primo: mes grandes angoisses métaphysiques
> Sont passées à l'état de chagrins domestiques;[6]

This, being addressed to the reader, sets a tone of apologetic defiance. We sense a personal tragedy half confessed, which it would be improper to probe. No love, no faith, above all no identity, no human nature to sustain the individual, "Qui ne croit à son Moi qu'à ses moments perdus."[7] Hence the costumes which give an identity, his central obsession.

Stevens, on the other hand, seldom allows himself to speak in the first person. Few are the personal references, fewer still the direct confessions in the sentimental vein which Laforgue sought to strangle with his ironic whip. Compare, for feeling and tone, Stevens' careful, qualified, humorous utterance of sadness:

> But I am, in any case,
> A most inappropriate man
> In a most unpropitious place.[8]

With Laforgue's poignant outcry:

> Oh! Rien à faire sur la terre![9]

[6] *Les Complaintes*, "Complainte d'une convalescence en mai," *Œuvres complètes*, I, 193.

[7] *Derniers Vers*, III; "Dimanches," *Œuvres complètes*, II, 151.

[8] *Ideas of Order*, "Sailing after Lunch."

[9] *Des Fleurs de bonne volonté*, XII, "Dimanches," *Œuvres complètes*, II, 30.

WALLACE STEVENS
and the Symbolist Imagination

Both are misfits, for whom life is "quotidian," a "malady," and Stevens assuredly borrowed the words and the pose from Laforgue. But there is a great difference between the latter's existential spleen and Stevens' dissatisfaction with "the common life." His "Disillusionment of Ten O'Clock" suggests remedies for the staleness of everything: color, dream, the life of the imagination. His ennui was Baudelaire's positive thirst for novelty, a powerful artistic motivation. "Why does one write poetry?" he asked in an essay; it is only "because one is impelled to do so by a personal sensibility and also because one grows tired of the monotony of one's imagination and sets out to find variety."[10] While Laforgue could never quite escape his bored self, Stevens did, by writing poetry about the positive value of poetic imagination, so that his poetry had for him, and still has for us, the virtues of an antidote against boredom. There was an invincible negation in Laforgue's spirit, an invincible affirmation in Stevens'. The affirmation presupposes the negation, so that in a sense the Laforguian pose mattered to Stevens as something to be overcome.

The positive good of the poetic imagination appears from first to last as the one central concern of Stevens' poetry. But it is only in retrospect that *Harmonium* is unified by this singleness of purpose. Even ten years after its appearance, it was a prophetic insight to realize that the "supreme fiction" of "To a High-Toned Old Christian Woman" would develop into the transcendental mystery explored by "Notes toward a Supreme Fiction," or that the heroic progeny of Hoon would by far outweigh the heirs to Crispin.

[10] "The Irrational Element in Poetry," *O.P.*, p. 221.

Pierrot, as he exists in *L'Imitation de Notre-Dame la lune*, manifests Laforgue's own attitude to art. It seems plausible that Stevens found in Pierrot the prototype of a clownish self-ironist representing the artist. But a census of Stevens' poetic heroes would not allow the parallel to be continued beyond his first book of verse. A sampling of four figures among his spokesmen will illustrate his evolution. The most Laforguian is certainly Carlos, from "Carlos among the Candles," a one-act play in the symbolist manner first published in 1917 and reprinted in *Opus Posthumous*. Curiously enough, Carlos wears Laforgue's own dandy's uniform: "He is dressed in black. He wears close-fitting breeches and a close-fitting, tightly-buttoned short coat. . . ." Like Pierrot, he is obsessed by the unconscious ("The causes of what I am are incalculable"), self-ironic ("truly, I am a modern"), oversophisticated ("silks and fans . . . the movements of arms, . . . rumors of Renoir . . . scorn of Debussy").[11] "Moi," says the original of Carlos, "je suis laminé d'esthétiques loyales."[12] But the snuffing of the candles at the end of the play recalls *Igitur* and the Mallarméan theory of imagination, a far cry from Laforgue. The second Pierrot character is Crispin, in "The Comedian as the Letter C." But his role in the capacity of a Romantic Ironist (Warren Ramsey's phrase) is very short; he goes through a sea-change and turns into a Realist; and one must agree with H. R. Hays that "there is in Stevens a philosophic evolution . . . which is typically New England and foreign to Laforgue."[13] If Pierrot is lunar,

[11] O.P., pp. 144-50.
[12] "Pierrots," *L'Imitation de Notre-Dame la lune*, Œuvres complètes, I, 231.
[13] RR, xxv (1934), 245.

WALLACE STEVENS
and the Symbolist Imagination

Crispin has both feet on earth. He belongs to the cynical, stoic, practical-minded lineage of comedy valets, from those of Lesage to those of Marivaux. The third personage is Hoon, a mythical hero, whose palingeneses are among the most exciting features of the *Collected Poems.*[14] There are nearly as many appearances of Hoon as there are of Pierrot in *L'Imitation,* the former as representative of Stevens as the latter of Laforgue. While "lord Pierrot" speaks in jest of his books, as the first Crispin did, Hoon embodies the magic of poetry. He is "lord of the land and lord / Of the men that live in the land, high lord."[15] He is a giant, a figure of nobility. Stevens has overcome, through the creation of this myth, the self-deprecation of his beginnings, when poetry was a secret vice. He can identify himself with the epiphanous vision of a poetic hero

> . . . large
> In my presence, the companion of presences
> Greater than mine, of his demanding, head
> And, of human realizings, rugged roy. . . .[16]

But Stevens never grows solemn about poetry. His hero has a fourth impersonation of Pierrot, or rather of Charlie Chaplin, the modern version. He comes at the end of the first section in "Notes toward a Supreme Fiction,"

---

[14] There are more than seven appearances: by name in "Tea at the Palaz of Hoon" (1921) and "Sad Strains of a Gay Waltz" (1935); as a recognizable figure in at least five other poems: "The Man with the Blue Guitar," "A Weak Mind in the Mountains," "A Rabbit as King of Ghosts," "Chocorua to Its Neighbor," and "A Primitive like an Orb."

[15] "Chocorua to Its Neighbor."   [16] "Chocorua to Its Neighbor."

> . . . in his old coat,
> His slouching pantaloons, beyond the town, . . .

He has the responsibility of "the final elegance," the supreme poem. This shows how, in a twist of the Pierrot theme, Stevens has reconciled the two traditions of Symbolism, the ironic and the serious. It is a matter for conjecture whether Laforgue's evolution, cut short by premature death, would have led beyond the Pierrot attitude to a less negative world-view. An opposition of temperament underlies Laforgue's need for a protective cloak and Stevens' adoption of the regalia of the poetic hero.

Stevens' poetry is a poetry of celebration. His praise of the moon, superficially allied to the Pierrot theme, has none of the death appeal which is its main characteristic in Laforgue; similarly his imitation of the Laforguian anti-solar invectives is not at all so certain as Ramsey hints. Both in the earlier and the later poems, praise greets "the comforts of the sun,"[17] the "gorgeous wheel,"[18] "the strength of the sun,"[19] "the ever-brightening origin,"[20] until "the self and the sun were one / And his poems, although makings of his self, / Were no less makings of the sun."[21] Stevens loved the sun, to him a symbol of reality, nearly as much as Laforgue hated it.

As soon as we pass from theme to manner, real correspondences begin to vibrate between the two poets, and

[17] "Sunday Morning," *Harmonium*.
[18] "Sailing after Lunch," *Ideas of Order*.
[19] "The Latest Freed Man," *Parts of a World*.
[20] "The Auroras of Autumn," iv, *The Auroras of Autumn*.
[21] "The Planet on the Table," *The Rock*.

these in turn illuminate whatever narrow fringes of their sensibilities may overlap.

An important reason why Stevens turned to Laforgue for a poetic manner is that he must have found in the French poet the first verbal expression of the Impressionist impulse. There is no proof of this, of course, beyond internal evidence; but a complete parallelism would include such facts as these: each poet had a strong visual imagination, and each a common Impressionist sensibility—i.e., a sensitiveness to the mobility of weather, to variations of light according to hour of day and time of year, and a concern with change which became a tenet of their esthetics. Just as Laforgue as a precursor defended the Impressionists, unaccepted then because they were too new, Stevens stood for them when they seemed *vieux jeu*. But while what the Frenchman wrote in *La Gazette des Beaux Arts* remains for us full of original insights about *plein-air* painting, the Impressionist eye, the new esthetics, etc., Stevens never went beyond an unsophisticated delight in the pictures of the French Impressionists.[22]

In poetic practice, Stevens seems the more truly Impressionistic of the two. Laforgue shunned the sunshine and disliked summer light; he wrote mostly of rain and wind, of night skies and November evenings; in contradiction to that of the open-air school which he extolled, his light is often filtered through the curtains of a shabby little flat, or through the stained-glass *rosace* of a church. Stevens, on the other hand, offers the typical Impressionist's delight in air and chameleon light playing with blue shadows, his palette

22 See chapter 1, fn. 5.

sparkles with the light tones of an open-air artist and his scenes have more mobility and naturalness than those of Laforgue, who was the first poet to transpose the devices of Impressionism into the verbal continuum. There is, however, a certain absoluteness of resemblance between some of Laforgue's and Stevens' landscapes; for example, "Couchant d'hiver" displays great feeling for the dynamism and coldness of a windy sky:

> A travers le lacis des branches dépouillées
> Dont l'eau-forte sabrait le ciel bleu-clair et froid.

Stevens worked in the same manner, but etching (not an Impressionist treatment) was replaced by quick brushwork:

> Weather by Franz Hals
> Brushed up by brushy winds in brushy clouds,
> Wetted by blue, colder for white.[23]

The metaphors come from the painter's trade: etching, brushwork. Nature is the painter. Baudelaire, while using pictures and old prints as primers for his imagination, had never gone so far in the sophistication of vocabulary. He was careful to hide the painter's tools, leaving only the quintessence of the picture. This sophistication impels Laforgue to compose a painting spatially in his verse, by making us aware of the frame, with the resulting tension between static and dynamic elements:

> C'était un très-au vent d'octobre paysage
> Que découpe, aujourd'hui dimanche, la fenêtre,
> Avec sa jalousie en travers, hors d'usage,

[23] "Notes toward a Supreme Fiction," I, vi, *Transport to Summer.*

WALLACE STEVENS
and the Symbolist Imagination

> Où sèche, depuis quand! une paire de guêtres
> Tachant de deux mals blancs ce glabre paysage.[24]

It has the cruelty of a Degas. But it is to Monet, not Degas, that Stevens is closest, as in "Sea Surface full of Clouds." The iridescent greens and blues of the "Water-lilies" seem reflected in his words; the framework of the five sections remains fixed like the outlines of a picture, while the subtle variations within that framework play the role of color changing with the angle of light; the five time-references heighten the impression of an instantaneous vision changed five times.

Laforgue's use of "broken color" in so far as hyphenated words of color can render Impressionist divisionism, is more than matched by Stevens. We recognize in Laforgue's "Blancs rose, lilas blancs," the same process of color mixing as in Stevens' more elaborate "red-blue, red-purple," found in one of the numerous poems which, somewhat like "Rosace en vitrail," explore the subjectivity of chromatic perception.

What Marc Eigeldinger wrote of Laforgue's imagery applies directly to Stevens.[25] Color never used for picturesque effects, but symbolically, to convey impressions; color symbols so often repeated that they constitute an abstract symbolic; an esthetic of the ephemeral achieving atmosphere by a wealth of concrete details: these were the Laforguian features which helped Stevens to exploit as a poet his affinity with Impressionism.

[24] "Complainte d'un autre dimanche," *Complaintes, Œuvres complètes,* I, 92.
[25] Cf. *Le Dynamisme de l'image dans la poésie française* (Neuchâtel, 1943), pp. 163-70.

Hays, in his pioneering article, explored rather sum-
marily the influence of Laforgue's imagery on Stevens. Ram-
sey noted how late it extends and quoted the image of the
casino found in "Academic Discourse in Havana." An earlier
example, the famous "Peter Quince at the Clavier," shows
a more complex assimilation of Laforguian imagery. The
poem is partly built on the analogy between sentiment,
especially love, and music—an analogy in the form of a
metaphor equating the heart with a stringed instrument. This
metaphor appears at least five times in *Sanglot* and *Com-
plaintes*. Let us compare "Sieste Eternelle" and "Peter
Quince":

Oh! viens, corps soyeux que j'adore	Here in this room, desiring you Thinking of your blue-shadowed silk
L'Archet qui sur nos nerfs pince ces tristes gammes	The basses of their beings throb In witching chords, and their thin blood Pulse pizzicati of Hossana.

Of course such musical images stem from Verlaine. But the
specific amplification by Stevens, integrating the image into
a vaster whole, shows a difference of scope between Laforgue,
whose irony sharpens and shortens the idea (we play the
same tune), and Stevens (the tune is the essence of beauty,
immortal in the body). At the close of the poem, he turns
Laforgue's fiddle into Mallarmé's viol, so that "Peter Quince"
begins like "Sieste Eternelle" and ends like "Sainte":

> Now, in its immortality, it plays
> On the clear viol of her memory,
> And makes a constant sacrament of praise.

WALLACE STEVENS
and the Symbolist Imagination

Stevens in "Peter Quince at the Clavier" has successfully wedded the ironic-realist with the romantic-idealist type of imagery. This balance is, however, not maintained throughout his poetry and one is surprised, in as late a poem as "Things of August" (first published in 1949), by fresh whiffs of Laforguian whimsy, ruined by the romantic counterweight: "The moon is a tricorn, / Waved in pale adieu." However, artistic metaphors of this kind become fewer in the later works. In a powerful article, Frank Doggett[26] has shown that Stevens' style evolved toward the indigenous tradition of aphoristic statement which includes colonial literature, Thoreau, Dickinson, and Frost. Stevens' later style, best exemplified by "An Ordinary Evening in New Haven" or "The Sail of Ulysses," is an "appositive" style based on the "noun-verb *to be*–noun" sentence pattern. More and more rarely does it derive its pungency from the Laforguian conceit, but oftener from the recognitions of a meditative mind moving inside "the plain sense of things."

When it comes to tone itself, comparisons between English and French arouse our suspicion. But there are common features emerging from common attitudes. Both Stevens and Laforgue are subtle double-dealers in the rhetoric of Romanticism.

Much of Stevens' exuberance and glitter can be traced back to Laforgue's experiments. The apostrophe, a device more romantic than classical and more French than English, seems to exist in high proportion in both writers. But they establish a distance from the romantic by their familiar-

[26] Frank Doggett, "Wallace Stevens' Later Poetry," *ELH*, xxv (June 1958), 137.

ity in apostrophe. "O soleil, bon soleil!" says one; "Master soleil" hails the other. Another common way of flouting the romantic "intoning" is to use mystical rhetoric ironically. This becomes clear if we compare Coleridge's address to the moon:

> Mild splendour of the various-vested Night![27]

with Laforgue's blasphemous take-off on the Marial Salutation:

> Je vous salue, Vierge des Nuits, plaine de glace . . .[28]

and Stevens' mocking "in magnificent measure":

> Mother of Heaven, regina of the clouds.[29]

Along this line, the typically Laforguian device of pricking a bubble of high-flown rhetoric with the sting of the commonplace is found in Stevens too. The first stanza of "To the One of Fictive Music" begins as a hymn with an invocation in Baudelaire's devotional-diabolic style:

> Sister and mother and diviner love,

and ends with the mildly humorous and wryly unparadoxical

> No crown is simpler than the simple hair.

The "hybridization of the Romantic," recognized by Stevens in Marianne Moore's "The Steeple-Jack" as a sign of the contemporaneous, is another Laforguian feature, exemplified particularly in his "Hamlet." It consists of a negative

[27] "Sonnet to the Autumnal Moon."
[28] "Lohengrin," *Moralités légendaires,* Paris, 1901, p. 77.
[29] "Le Monocle de Mon Oncle."

enumeration of the Romantic paraphernalia. From Crispin, "the poetic hero without regalia," to the angel of reality who says, in "Angel Surrounded by Paysans,"

> I have neither ashen wing nor wear of ore
> And live without a tepid aureole,

this hybridization is constant, an anti-rhetoric, the begrudging heir to romantic style.

Parody, a genre which received its nineteenth-century consecration in *L'Album zutique*, was used by Corbière and Laforgue as a tool of literary debunking directed at the Romantics and Parnassians. Stevens was certainly keen enough in French to enjoy Corbière's pastiche of Hugo's "Oceano Nox" or to detect Flaubert's Saint-Julien l'Hospitalier in Laforgue's Hamlet. He, too, parodied the Romanticists, sometimes with cruelty, as in "Mozart 1935," a discordant counterpoint to the "Ode to the West Wind":

> Be thou the voice,
> Not you. Be thou, be thou
> The voice of angry fear,
> The voice of this besieging pain.

And in "It Must Change," the second section of "Notes Toward a Supreme Fiction," this startling transformation of Shelley again:

> Bethou me, said sparrow, to the crackled blade,
> And you, and you, bethou me as you blow,
> When in my coppice you behold me be.
>
> Ah, ke! the bloody wren, the felon jay,
> Ke-ke, the jug-throated robin pouring out,
> Bethou, bethou, bethou me in my glade.

> There was such idiot minstrelsy in rain,
> So many clappers going without bells,
> That these bethous compose a heavenly gong.

This irony is of the French type; it kills with a smile. Both Eliot and Pound have accustomed their readers to ironic effects derived from judicious quotations, many of them foreign, but they seldom mock the meat they feed on. Laforgue's fastidiousness is quite different from their cultural appetite. His quotations are more the mark of an overfed *lettré* than of an eager universalist. For a change of diet, he would pun in German and English. Stevens' use of French has the same cause, weariness, and the same effect, a freshening up:

> Natives of poverty, children of malheur,
> The gaiety of language is our seigneur.[30]

He went as far as venturing five whole lines in French, woven into the admirable fabric of "Sea Surface Full of Clouds." Placed in strategic position at the very fulcrum of each section, they are quite effective and have attracted much critical commentary. Their uncertain scansion (three undecasyllabics, a very awkward meter, and two decasyllabics with irregular pauses) has not prevented hyperbolic comparisons with French poets. These lines combine demotic terms of endearment ("mon bijou," "mon âme," etc.) with ironic sentimentality into what eventually may sound somewhat like Baudelaire. But not the best Baudelaire; rather like a Baudelaire pastiched by a Laforgue.

What Ezra Pound defined as the "logopoeia" in Laforgue's

---

[30] "Esthétique du Mal," xi, *Transport to Summer.*

verse, a dance of the intellect among words, was also found by H. R. Hays in *Harmonium*. Later works continuously evince the same joy in the dangerous powers of language. Dangerous because metaphysical coinages are not always beautiful; we learn that Laforgue, the artist overcoming the prankster in him, tried to eradicate his neologisms, such as *sangsuelles* and *sexciproques*, from galley proofs.[31] Among the funny, but ugly, adverbs coined by him, this international creation of Stevens' would not sound squeamish:

> The grackles sing avant the spring
> Most spiss—oh! Yes, most spissantly.[32]

The ding-dongs in the same poem and in a score of others, rich, perhaps cloyed, with onomatopoeia, echo the bim-bam of the *Complainte des cloches* rather than Poe's tintinnabulations. Poe was humorless; Stevens made the most of his freedom, gained thanks to the French. Corbière and Rimbaud had waged war on the traditional harmonies, each in his own wild way. Laforgue in turn was liberated and passed on the new music to the Surrealists. Some of Stevens' feats of auditory humor could also be blamed on Lewis Carroll's nursery rhymes, the only successful attempt at stream-of-consciousness nonsense in English poetry before E. E. Cummings. But the common trait of Laforgue and Stevens is that their nonsense is never meaningless, and this justifies both Pound's illuminating phrase and our parallelism.

Rhythmic patterns can hardly be compared from one language to another. Stevens is on the whole very conserva-

---

[31] Cf. Marie-Jeanne Durry, *Jules Laforgue*, Paris, 1952, p. 162.
[32] "Esthétique du Mal," xi, *Transport to Summer*.

tive, Wordsworthian, and Shelleyan in his use of verse. But some departures from the three lines unrhymed and arranged in waves, which increasingly became his chief rhythmic cluster, look very much like Laforgue's free verse, as distinguished from Gustave Kahn's *vers libre*. There is the same stanzaic freedom, syntactical control, and natural use of repetition in "Domination of Black" as in "Solo de Lune." Apart from what concerns stanzas, the same still holds for "Song of Fixed Accord," an experiment published thirty years later. To know whether Stevens learned his little used free verse from fellow-Imagists or directly from Laforgue would only shift the influence from first to second hand. "Derniers vers" have certainly had extraordinary significance for the poet who wrote "Burghers of Petty Death,"

> In which a wasted figure, with an instrument,
> Propounds blank, final music.

Influence is as elusive and complex a notion as that of environment or heredity. Kinship or affinity seem the only words the critic can use, especially in the relationship between Stevens and Laforgue; even now the letters of Wallace Stevens have been published, there is nothing he can avail himself of in the way of external evidence. But the kinship exists, not so much of *soul* as of *art*.

This dichotomy is perfectly possible. Stevens was not "the poor young man," the "chronic orphan" that Laforgue was. He grew to be a celebrant of the earth and of poetry. Yet his irony always kept him safe from romantic fervor. He shared with Laforgue a will not to be, *qua* artist, the dupe of his own rhetoric. Coming of literary age one full genera-

WALLACE STEVENS
and the Symbolist Imagination

tion after Laforgue (although he was born only nineteen years after him and his first readable publications appeared only thirteen years after the influential first edition of the *Œuvres complètes de Jules Laforgue* [1901–1903]), Stevens' position was different; and the difference widened with time. Laforgue, encouraged by Rimbaud's war cry, fought the first battle against the rational; Stevens chants the victory of the nonrational. Bergson and Santayana and Croce had toppled Taine and Comte for him, Taine and Comte against whom Laforgue's only combat ram was the then little known works of Hartmann. To these conditions must be added divergences of temperament, Laforgue's toward a negative and Stevens' toward a more positive view of life. This partly explains their jarring attitudes towards the value of poetry. Laforgue never felt poetry as apotheosis. He covered his lack of confidence with the mask of a dandified Pierrot. Stevens used Charlie Chaplin's clown as a mask for his own sense of aggrandizement and nobility.

Many parallels of technique intersect in the non-Euclidian geometry of literary influence; they focus on the importance of Laforgue for any assessment of Stevens' manner. The mobility of the Hartford skies and the delight in Monet's pictures combined with the reading of Laforgue to create a unique literary expression of the Impressionist impulse and sensibility. Perhaps a clearer example of the strengthening of a basic trend by the influence of two different arts could not be found in literature; yet, if one looks around a little, particularly in the post-romantic domain, he may not think such a relationship uncommon.

[1959]

3

Baudelaire and Mallarmé

Beyond the knowledge of nakedness, as part
Of reality, beyond the knowledge of what
Is real, part of a land beyond the mind. . . .

("Extracts from Addresses to the Academy
of Fine Ideas")

THE STARTING POINT of this inquiry is a stanza of "Extracts from Addresses to the Academy of Fine Ideas":

> Where is that summer warm enough to walk
> Among the lascivious poisons, clean of them,
> And in what covert may we, naked, be
> Beyond the knowledge of nakedness, as part
> Of reality, beyond the knowledge of what
> Is real, part of a land beyond the mind?

While the first half of this quotation superabounds with echoes and fragrances from Baudelaire, the second half has in intent, if not in style, the ascetic character of Mallarmé's quest. With the first we associate the nostalgic tone of:

> J'aime le souvenir de ces époques nues . . .[1]

and:

> Au milieu de l'azur, des vagues, des splendeurs
> Et des esclaves nus, tout imprégnés d'odeur . . .[2]

With Mallarmé's search for an absolute poetry, we associate Stevens' use of words which he may have learned from the French master: "knowledge," "nakedness," "beyond." But we soon become dissatisfied with our associations. Whatever sameness struck us at first pales in the glare of essential differences. Baudelaire remembers nature before the fall; Stevens projects his Adamic hopefulness.[3] Mallarmé seeks a

---

[1] Charles Baudelaire, *Œuvres complètes*, Paris, 1931, p. 87.

[2] Charles Baudelaire, "La Vie antérieure," *Œuvres complètes*, p. 93.

[3] This essay was written in part to answer a question asked by Roy Harvey Pearce in *The Continuity of American Poetry*, Princeton, 1961, p. 7. I took cognizance of his brilliant history of the Adamic tradition after publishing an article in *Critique*, XVII (December 1961), "Sur le

WALLACE STEVENS
and the Symbolist Imagination

land of the mind beyond reality; Stevens a land beyond the mind, as part of reality. Because of such exchanges among words and symbols shared by Baudelaire, Stevens, and Mallarmé, parallelisms must be checked out beneath their words, at the boundaries of their imaginary worlds.

One motive for metaphor has to do with clothing, concealment, protection, placation. It metamorphoses the world into pleasurable likenesses, multiplies its colors, its perfumes, and its sounds, yet stresses their profound unity. In poetry of this kind, the images enhance bodily well-being, the value of nutrition, the feminine presences of Night, Moon, and Earth, in their maternal role of dispelling fear. The imagination successfully creates a world whose vitality does not deny, but veils or beautifies, death's finality. The lyric dictionary of such an imagination enters phrases like "éternelle chaleur" and "eternal bloom" (Baudelaire's in "La Chevelure"; Stevens' in "Le Monocle de Mon Oncle"). It is romantic by its arrest of time. Its rhetoric makes of metaphor the chief vehicle of its discoveries especially by use of the synecdoche which creates a world within a world, as though language had the same innate fecundity as Nature. Its poetics welcome lexical opulence. Its aesthetics have, since Baudelaire found their name, Correspondances. Its religion is a mystic humanism, hedonistic rather than heroic. The poetry of the beautiful surface with the dark terror beneath does not, however, escape the facts of death and suffering. It is a means of overcoming terror. Hence the invention of the gods and the worship of the imagination.

Prétendu Symbolisme de Wallace Stevens," dissociating Stevens from the French tradition.

Harmonium, and some poems of *Les Fleurs du Mal*, will admit the reader through a passage going down[4] into the secure interiors of a world of "indulgences." But we must qualify the oversimplified view of Stevens as a hedonist. In fact, as Richard Ellmann has suggested it,[5] death is the constant obsession of the poet from the first[6] to the last. In

[4] The psychic history of modern man starts with the matriarchal consciousness which rests in large part on *participation mystique* with natural environment (Erich Neumann, *The Great Mother*, second ed. New York 1963, p. 293). In this stage "the human psyche and the extra-human world were still largely undivided" (*ibid.*). Lunar mythology from all parts of the world records the precedence of the moon as life-giver over the sun. "In astral mythology the moon has an upperworld character and the sun an underworld character" (p. 314). This pattern still underlay the patriarchal motif of the Eleusinian mysteries, but in the patriarchal stage the sun became the dominant and positive symbol. The moon suffers a marriage of death with the sun. In Christianity the mythological figure of the suffering moon woman became *luna patiens*. She is still the archetype of the Great Mother, and Ernst Robert Curtius has shown how she entered medieval literature through Bernard Sylvestris' *Universitate Mundi*. The moon is "the midpoint of the Golden Chain, navel of the upper and lower worlds" (E. R. Curtius, *European Literature and the Latin Middle Ages*, New York 1953, p. 108). It is in the sky and within us. Furthermore, this movement inward and down by which the patriarchal consciousness experiences the moon is also a movement backward toward maternal origins. Bernard Sylvestris' theory of "correspondances" is an emanation of the archetype of the Great Mother. The Macrocosm is *in* the Microcosm (Cf. Baudelaire: "La Nature est un temple . . ."). It is the paradox of *Correspondantia*, as also apprehended by John Senior (*The Way Down and Out*, Ithaca, N.Y. 1959). The *Symbolistes' askesis* perhaps continued this development, as they fought free of the lunar *participation mystique* (or "correspondances" realized as lunacy).

[5] Richard Ellmann, "Wallace Stevens' Ice-cream," *Kenyon Review*, (Winter 1957).

[6] Samuel French Morse relates that in 1918 Stevens had a conversation about death with Miss Harriet Monroe, and said that "the sub-

WALLACE STEVENS
and the Symbolist Imagination

Harmonium, almost no poem dodges the theme, almost none refuses to minister the solace of poetry, only a few face the fact of death with derision or dirge.

During the late twenties a change occurred in Stevens' imagery. He summarized this change in "Farewell to Florida," consciously placing this poem, written in 1936, at the threshold of his new *Ideas of Order.* True, all its themes were already in *Harmonium;* yet too much cannot be made of the poet's self-realization. Quite lucidly, he stated that for him the imagination of Night, with its constellating images of the South, the Moon-Woman, vegetation, summer, nature, music, must give way to the masculine constellation of Day, North, men, mud, winter, society, and violence. Thus, he was making his adjustment to reality, which now included misery for millions, the Depression, the impending world catastrophe. The change of symbols entailed a change of style. The very structure of the poem tells us that the protected world of the synecdoche has been abandoned for the fight of mind against chaos. Antithesis, both in composition and syntax, produces a poetry of "ghostlier demarcations," "contrary theses," sharp light effects. A new motive for the poet's craft appears, the pursuit of a knowledge of reality. The aesthetics of "order" makes a cleavage between "reality" and "imagination" in spite of "their incessant conjunctionings."[7] The theme of nakedness took hold of Stevens' imagination during this period, perhaps under the influence of Mallarmé's ascetic

---

ject absorbed him." See "Lettres d'un Soldat," *Dartmouth College Bulletin,* v (December 1961), p. 50.

[7] Statement on the dust-jacket of *Ideas of Order,* New York, 1936.

example. As the opposition of word and world grew in his mind, Stevens yearned for transparence. Metaphor cloaks reality. The image of green leaves covering the "basic slate" of death changes into the image of veils that must be stripped. Hence a tendency toward the abstract, a refining of poetic vocabulary. But Stevens, even at his wintriest, never followed Mallarmé's rarities, and kept something of his original gaiety and bigness of diction. The symbols of the sun, light, air, mountain-tops, and hero now constellate in a poetry of pure sight, of sight purified by poetry. The dreams of heroic humanism soar up, and their verticality lends to them a moral meaning somewhat absent in *Harmonium*. The poetry of divestment and naked sight even takes on a collective significance when both Stevens and Mallarmé envisage a "supreme fiction." These are the common directions; many are the divergences.

The imagination's sex, always androgynous in all poets, follows the dialectics of animus and anima. Primitive androgyneity, Stevens' later poetry seems to say, is the absolute poetic state, the mystic equilibrium.[8] The final result of the "up and down between" sun and moon, is a happy marriage between the giant projection of the masculine self and the earth-spouse; it is a cyclic gesture unifying season with season and world with word, a marriage and a cycle whose stylistic icon is often Stevens' repetitive pattern of three-line stanzas, as opposed to Mallarmé's hieratic tombstones.

[8] Stevens knew and used Jung's terminology, "anima" and "animus"; e.g., "His anima liked its animal" in a passage about the maternal archetype. *C.P.*, p. 322.

WALLACE STEVENS
and the Symbolist Imagination

This is of course an abstract schema—but voluntarily so, because our endeavor is to trace the polarity veiling-nakedness through the inner space, symbolism, and poetics of Stevens and his French confreres.

Stevens and Baudelaire

> This old, black dress,
> I have been embroidering
> French flowers on it.[9]

Recent phenomenological criticism[10] has disengaged at least three Baudelaires from the complex formula: "De la concentration et de la vaporisation du Moi, tout est là" (Mon Coeur mis à nu). To which was Stevens attentive? To the poet of nature's infinite dilation (symbolized by the sea, perfumes, far horizons), whose very dissemination in space brought about the anguish of emptiness and dissolution? Or to the poet who fought the vertigo of expansion

[9] "Explanation," C.P., p. 72. Imagination "embroiders" on the black dress: death is old, permanent. The flowers are fragile, but they add color, in the way a French word does to a sentence. They are artificial, not natural flowers. William York Tindall quotes this poem in his *Wallace Stevens*, Minneapolis, 1961, p. 15, and we should follow his advice to read alongside it Baudelaire's "Éloge du Maquillage."

[10] Chiefly J.-P. Richard, *Poésie et Profondeur*, Paris, 1955, and G. Poulet, *Les Métamorphoses du Cercle*, Paris, 1961. I disagree with their attempt to turn Baudelaire into a poet of infinite space. No "solar tropism" verticalizes Baudelaire's dreams. In fact, as Gaston Bachelard pointed out, he was a terrestrial, not an aerial, poet (*L'Air et les Songes*, Paris, 1960, p. 158). Stevens, on the contrary, partook in the "Nietzschean imagination" of pure air, and did not need to translate space in terms of depth and swimming, as Baudelaire always did.

and natural fecundity (symbolized by the teeming carrion), and fought it by a thickening, almost a solidification of the self, to the point of immobility: art giving this counternatural fixity? Or, again, was Stevens attentive to the Baudelaire who conjugated the two movements into one, and whose imagined paradise combined the memory of limitless space within the protective shell of the temple, the ship, the island, the sky felt as a cup?

It is difficult to answer on behalf of Wallace Stevens, because he limited his allusions to and borrowings from Baudelaire to a few excerpts (e.g., "my semblables" transferred from "Au lecteur" to "Dutch Graves in Bucks County"), one or two parodies (e.g., the five French lines in "Sea Surface Full of Clouds") a pronouncement on the aesthetics of decreation at the end of *The Necessary Angel*, and the beautiful analysis of the opening lines of "La Vie Antérieure," which is perhaps the most revealing published document of his way of reading French Poetry.[11] Stevens' comments show him a keen and sympathetic judge of Baudelaire's imaginary experience. The kind of sympathy which Stevens evinces is akin to an affinity. It is a sympathy which enabled Stevens to feel the importance to Baudelaire of the phrase "au milieu de l'azur," rendered by "at the *centre* of azure" and of the "vast porticoes," endowed by Stevens with more than casual or romantic value:

We stand looking at a remembered habitation. All old dwelling-places are subject to these transmogrifications and

11 O.P., pp. 202-16.

WALLACE STEVENS

and the Symbolist Imagination

the experience of all of us includes a succession of old dwelling-places: abodes of the imagination, ancestral or memories of places that never existed.[12]

Quite rightly, Stevens was tuning his ear to a theme which is rather easy to miss in Baudelaire's more expansive moods. Critics miss it, who pick up only the Wagnerian melody of "expansion infinie." But even that most hackneyed of all romantic images, "la nature est un temple," possesses the charm of "a remembered habitation." It is a pity that few critics ever mention that the sonnet "Correspondances" is the recounting of a hashish dream. The "temple" of the first line, with its "living pillars" speaking "garbled words" and casting "familiar glances" to man, is the "transmogrification" of a remembered habitation, an artificial paradise, as a matter of fact probably a friend's room.[13] No wonder,

[12] *O.P.*, p. 204.

[13] My proof for this unorthodox view comes from two prose texts by Baudelaire: "Du Vin et du haschisch," 1851, and "Le poème du haschisch," 1858 (*Œuvres complètes*, pp. 409-477.) In the first, he wrote: "Les hallucinations commencent. . . . Les sons ont une couleur, les couleurs ont une musique. . . . Les peintures du plafond . . . prennent une vie effrayante. . . . Toute contradiction est devenue unité. L'homme est *passé* dieu." In the second, the ceiling becomes a vault, then a cage: "Je me considérais comme enfermée pour long-temps, pour des milliers d'années peut-être, dans cette cage somptueuse, au milieu de ces paysages féeriques, entre ces horizons merveilleux. . . ." Then the "living pillars" and "familiar looks" appear: "Mais toutes les divinités mythologiques [allegorical figures painted on the walls of the room] me regardaient avec un charmant sourire. . . ." The same pattern appears in the next dream: a ceiling deepens, painted figures look understandingly, symbols and synesthesias develop: "Les peintures du *plafond* revêtiront une vie effrayante; les plus grossiers papiers peints qui tapissent les *murs* des auberges se creuseront comme de splendides

then, that there should be so few instances of "correspond-ances" (apart from the rather trite device of synesthesia) in Baudelaire's poetry as a whole. These mystic moments re-quired a "temple" and the intoxication caused by a drug, or their substitutes: an alcove and a woman's perfume. In no case did the vistas of outdoor nature—suggested by a casual reading of "Correspondances"—produce the conditions of the experience. Baudelaire's paradise was the transfiguration of trivial details printed on wallpaper; his sky, a ceiling deepened by imagination; his synesthesia, a real sound or sight fragranced by hallucination. To him, paradise had the ambiguous shape of a cage: a temple, pillars, vast porticoes, that retain the poet's self while it expands. Nature was dreamed from a room, the walls of which receded to the controlled depths of dioramas. "Expansion infinie" yes, but within a "temple."[14]

In "La Chevelure," a perfume signals the inward move-

---

dioramas. Les nymphes aux chairs éclatantes vous *regardent* avec de grands yeux plus profonds et plus limpides que le ciel et l'eau; les personnages de l'antiquité . . . échangent avec vous par le simple *regard* de solennelles confidences. . . . Cependant se développe cet état mystérieux et temporaire de l'esprit, où la *profondeur* de la vie . . . se révèle *tout entière* dans le spectacle . . . qu'on a sous les yeux— où le premier objet venu devient *symbole parlant.* Fourier et Sweden-borg, l'un avec ses *analogies,* l'autre avec ses *correspondances,* se sont incarnés dans le végétal et l'animal qui tombent sous votre regard, et au lieu d'enseigner par la voix, ils vous endoctrinent par la forme et par la couleur. . . ."

[14] In his book on symbolism, *Des Métaphores obsédantes au mythe personnel,* Paris, 1963, Charles Mauron has suggested an even bolder meaning: "L'analogie universelle est la clé magique qui permet la pos-session intérieure de la mère, le contrôle de sa réalité" (p. 142).

WALLACE STEVENS
and the Symbolist Imagination

ment by which Baudelaire discovers a larger world within the
happy vessel of his paradise:

> Je plongerai ma tête amoureuse d'ivresse
> Dans ce noir océan où l'autre est enfermé
> Et mon esprit subtil que le roulis caresse
> Saura vous retrouver, ô féconde paresse,
> Infinis bercements du loisir embaumé!

By deepening a sea and a sky inside his mistress's black hair,
then peopling it with bright sails, lazy cradling motions,
eternal warmth, the poet turned into pleasure his habitual
sense of the inner void. His desire for a *plenum* was fulfilled
by an imaginative paradox well known to the mystics. The
large in the small is discovered through metaphors of con-
tainment. A hemisphere is contained in a woman's hair, a
macrocosm in a microcosm, a world of images in a draft
of wine, the wine in the woman-bottle. At the core of the
imagination of "correspondances," the vessel archetype man-
ages the successive sensual discoveries of "La Chevelure."

The same imagination of prenatal comfort and aesthetic
pleasure links Stevens with the spirit of Baudelaire's "cor-
respondances." The image "The high interiors of the sea"
recurs in contexts reminiscent of the exotic settings of "La
Chevelure" or "La Vie Antérieure." Exoticism in Stevens
and Baudelaire followed an inward movement. For instance,
"ce noir océan où l'autre est enfermé" corresponds with
"Jasmine's Beautiful Thoughts underneath the Willow," a
dream

> Of bliss submerged beneath appearance,
> In an interior ocean's rocking
> Of long, capricious fugues and chorals. (*C.P.* 79)

Although Stevens warns us that his "titillations have no foot-notes," the image seems incomplete without the pedantic gloss that the willow is the symbolic tree of Hecate, the goddess of death. It is she who, in "Sunday Morning," "makes the willow shiver in the sun." She is the secret which Baudelaire and Stevens share, the common denominator of their paradisial poetry. For at the end of "La Vie Antérieure," Baudelaire hints at "the grievous secret that made [me] pine." Hashish, drunkenness, art, were the best *veils* (his word) to fill the inner void, the giddy tomb hollowed within him, or at least to hide it. The imagination, at its most expansive in "Correspondances," seemed to Baudelaire man's best protection against the vast spaces ready to engulf him. But mothered by Madame Aupick and a Jansenist tradition, his vivid imagery of death often overpowered the maternal archetype.

There are very few "fecundity" images in Baudelaire, in contrast to Stevens. If I have pleasure in imagining that my body corresponds limb for limb with the World's Body, it is because nature is both beautiful and good. But Baudelaire could imagine nature as a bountiful mother only in a remote past, before the Fall:

> Du temps que la Nature en sa verve puissante
> Concevait chaque jour des enfants monstrueux,
> J'eusse aimé vivre auprès d'une jeune géante,
> Comme au pied d'une reine un chat voluptueux.[15]

Fecundity and poetry, creation and speech: close companions. Baudelaire nostalgically fuses them in a pun.[16] Verve

---

[15] Baudelaire, "La Géante," *Œuvres complètes*, p. 97.
[16] Pointed out by Judd D. Hubert in *L'Esthétique des* Fleurs du Mal, Geneva, 1953.

and Verb both created, in some "anterior" world which was, we know, also an "interior" world. But those times were ended by some corruption of Nature, probably the appearance of death. The giant queen whose speech could create, the feminine archetype as Nature, no longer allows the poet to nestle in her lap. The only communication he has with her bounty is through the hallucinations of hashish and the vessel-imagery of "Correspondances."

Stevens' poetry, on the contrary, has its generating center in the archetype. All but six poems of *Harmonium* exemplify the maternal role of the imagination. The six exceptions are: "The Snow Man," "The Emperor of Ice-Cream," "The Bird with the Keen, Coppery Claws," "Tea at the Palaz of Hoon," "New England Verses," and possibly "Anatomy of Monotony": they announce the sun-style to come.

Early critics of Stevens' hedonism have generally failed to see the tragic darkness which underlies the gorgeous colors and funny little sounds of *Harmonium*. "The quirks of imagery," as we read in Stevens' exemplary poem of "swallowing," "Frogs Eat Butterflies. Snakes Eat Frogs. Hogs Eat Snakes. Men Eat Hogs," are there because "the night is not the cradle that they cry." The night is hostile, and imagination safeguards us. The moon is one of its inventions. She is "mother of pathos and pity"[17] and her counterpart the candle will even outlast her as a symbol of the imagination: the "valley candle" of *Harmonium* still shines in *The Rock*, when the moon has long ago failed because it is too ambiguous. The lamp in a child's room

[17] C.P., p. 107.

remained associated with the tales which Stevens loved, and
with images of protection:

> Within its vital boundary, in the mind.
> We say God and the imagination are one . . .
> How high that highest candle lights the dark.

> Out of this same light, out of the central mind,
> We make a dwelling in the evening air,
> In which being there together is enough.[18]

The insistence on the role of the imagination, even the sym-
bolism of the light in the dark,[19] and the impulse toward

[18] *C.P.*, p. 524.
[19] Cf. "Les Phares" in which painters are compared to beacons in
the abysmal night. Also, "Le Voyage": "Ah! que le monde est grand
à la clarté des lampes!" This poem may have influenced Stevens, who
may have noted Baudelaire's ambiguous attitude toward the imagina-
tion, as a safeguard against *ennui*, as a means to *renew* our world. By
"Au fond de l'inconnu pour trouver du nouveau," does Baudelaire
mean the same things as Stevens: "We accept the unknown even when
we are most skeptical"? (*O.P.*, p. 288) Stevens' worship of imagina-
tion, in "Disillusionment of Ten O'Clock," for instance, is less miti-
gated than Baudelaire's:

> O le pauvre amoureux des pays chimériques!
> Faut-il le mettre aux fers, le jeter à la mer,
> Ce matelot ivrogne, inventeur d'Amériques
> Dont le mirage rend le gouffre plus amer? (Le Voyage)

as compared with:

> Only, here and there, an old sailor,
> Drunk and asleep in his boots,
> Catches tigers
> In red weather. (Disillusionment of Ten O'Clock)

Of this image, Howard Baker wrote it was "interesting in itself but
nonsignificant" ("Wallace Stevens," *The Achievement of Wallace*

WALLACE STEVENS
and the Symbolist Imagination

the vessel are of the same imaginary type as Baudelaire's. The difference is in the metaphysics of the "central mind." For Stevens the imagination has no extra-human source, and "the world imagined" (by man) "is the ultimate good." It is a world shored up by the miracle of imagery against the vital fears of night. Thus the birds of black which haunted the "walker in the moonlight"[20] became in another poem "euphemized" into thirteen blackbirds, all except one concealing the terror they evoked.[21] The abysmal night of chaos still gapes in the gloom of "Heaven considered as a Tomb," and it recalls another side of Baudelaire, the poet of gnawing worms and icy hells.

But it would be a mistake to compare "The Worms at Heaven's Gate" to "Une Charogne." In Stevens' poem, the imagination conquers the horror of death by a sea-change. No foul smell or teeming infection; the irony comes from the subtle tension between separation and wholeness: death as itemization versus life as organism. The wit of Stevens carries the theme of swallowing even into the name, Badroul-ba-dour, even into the syntax: "we her chariot."[22]

Much more successfully than Baudelaire, Stevens can master night:

> The night is the color
> Of a woman's arm:

Stevens, New York, 1963, p. 88). If it has its genesis in Baudelaire, it expresses a much more positive attitude toward imagination in general.

[20] C.P., p. 77.

[21] Directly opposed to Ellmann's interpretation of the blackbird as the force of life.

[22] C.P., p. 49.

Night, the female,
Obscure,
Fragrant and supple,
Conceals herself.[23]

Stevens' night hides the original dark with colors which are euphemizations of black, mostly green and purple. Elsewhere (*Collected Poems*, pp. 223, 267), he repeats that "Green is the night" . . . "the archaic queen." Thus among the symbols of vestment and concealment used by Stevens, foliage plays a major role. Be it Pennsylvania's green or Florida's green the color is dreamed in depth as well as perceived. It is an emanation of the archetype, the product of natural fecundity, as well as the "fictive covering" which man's imagination disposes over the "basic slate," the bare rock of fact and death. In *Harmonium*, the darkness remains precariously kept under control. "Domination of Black" presents a notable exception to the color symbolism of the book, in which statistically green is first (43), blue second (28), white third (21), then gold (20), black, dark, and purple (14 each), red (12) and yellow (7). "Green is the night" . . . and green the "fusky alphabet" taught "Phosphor" by "that elemental parent."[24]

A Sears, Roebuck list of Stevens' symbols would just catalogue his favorite garments; he loved sombreros. But basic movements of the mind reveal more than its inventory. In *Harmonium* the reflex to cloak expresses a relationship between clothes and language, between language and the clothes which language weaves, almost like leaves and almost like fabric, at once manmade and natural. The gowns of

[23] *C.P.*, p. 73.   [24] *C.P.*, p. 267.

WALLACE STEVENS
and the Symbolist Imagination

grammarians are like "the speech of clouds,"[25] the theme of embroidery parallels the efforts of the imagination,[26] cloak-moon-singer is a recurrent cluster[27] and in spite of Crispin's decision, taken late in the development of *Harmonium,* to "lay bare" his "cloudy drift," to tear the veils of Spring "irised in dew and early fragrancies" and to seek "a sinewy nakedness,"[28] we shall see this dual symbolism of fecundity and language persist throughout Stevens' poetry. In fact this relationship may have been what he grasped of the rapport between poetry and reality, when at the end of "Notes toward a Supreme Fiction" he called by name his muse, the archetype, "Fat girl, terrestrial . . . my green, my fluent mundo."[29] The earth is green, round, maternal, fecund—an image seldom found in Baudelaire's poems, but present in Stevens'. To the end, the imagination of covering will resist the intelligence of divestment:

> Then Ozymandias said the spouse, the bride
> Is never naked. A fictive covering
> Weaves always glistening from the heart and mind.[30]

The happy color, green, the reticular web secreted by the imagination, joins man with nature, the fecund woman.

Dandyism, our second parallel, attaches a good deal of importance to sartorial symbols. It interests us as a signal of aesthetic feeling rather than as an aspect of politics. Gorham Munson, its inventor, brilliantly forestalled Jean-Paul Sartre's analysis[31] when he noted the difference between "the metallic

[25] *C.P.*, p. 55.   [26] *C.P.*, pp. 72, 84, 64.   [27] *C.P.*, pp. 57, 74.
[28] *C.P.*, p. 36.   [29] *C.P.*, pp. 406-07.   [30] *C.P.*, p. 396.
[31] Jean-Paul Sartre, *Baudelaire*, Paris, 1947, p. 161: "Le dandysme baudelairien est une réaction personnelle au problème de la situation sociale de l'écrivain."

shell secreted by a restless man against a despised social order" and Stevens' "well-fed, well-booted dandyism of contentment," which, he added, reminded him of "the America of baronial estates."[32] It was a remarkable judgment, especially in view of its date, 1925. Hindsight makes us more cautious, however. As early as 1920, Stevens' poetic hero cut a much less impeccable figure than we were led to believe. We read in "Anecdote of the Abnormal":

> Crispin-valet, Crispin-saint!
> The exhausted realist beholds
> His tattered manikin arise,
> Tuck in the straw,
> And stalk the skies.[33]

This announced the rejection of "regalia" by the Comedian, and a succession of ragged figures, who, in self-irony, projected Stevens' image of the ideal poet! At mid-point down the line of heroes, the virile young poet, poorly dressed and intent on the sun, won in an aesthetic see-saw over an elegant lady, whose dress and moonlight were one ("Mrs. Alfred Uruguay"). It was clear that an essential redefinition of elegance was in process, and Stevens' by now familiar cosmic symbols (repeated in "The Well Dressed Man with a Beard": "No was the night. Yes is this present sun") lent general meaning to the reversal. All these imaginary functions converged: the sun, light, the eye, the masculine hero, and nakedness as a mode of knowing. The "final elegance" was to be reserved for the Chaplinesque figure at the end of

[32] Gorham Munson, "The Dandyism of Wallace Stevens" in *The Achievement of Wallace Stevens*, p. 43.

[33] *O.P.*, p. 24.

WALLACE STEVENS
and the Symbolist Imagination

"It Must Be Abstract," in "Notes toward a Supreme Fiction," proof that a clown, not a dandy, was the destination of Stevens' masks; now metaphysics gone, man stands alone:

> Cloudless the morning. It is he. The man
> In that old coat, those sagging pantaloons,
>
> It is of him, ephebe, to make, to confect
> The final elegance . . . .[34]

What do the dandy's clothes mean? To Baudelaire, the meaning is spiritual. The Symbolistic *askesis* stems from his series of articles in *Curiosités Esthétiques* as directly as from any other single source. "Dandyism is akin to spiritualism and stoicism."[35] The latter word justifies Munson's analysis; the former suggests something else, perhaps a purification. The next article says in effect: the natural female is abominable, but a fashionable woman is a dandy's love "fusing both woman and the dress into an indivisible totality."[36] In the next article, Baudelaire progresses to the praise of make-up, which brings the human body closer to the immobility of a statue: "idole, elle doit se *dorer* pour être adorée . . . pour consolider et diviniser (sa) fragile beauté."[37] Art receives the task of hardening the shell of human appearance, in order to create a supernatural and magic being, indivisible from its dress, whose flesh becomes, so to speak, materialized by the artifice. A refusal of change, of time? Perhaps something more: a need to fill the inner space with substance, or

[34] *C.P.*, p. 389.
[35] Baudelaire, *Œuvres complètes*, p. 907.
[36] Baudelaire, *Œuvres complètes*, p. 910.
[37] Baudelaire, *Œuvres complètes*, p. 913.

to contain its expansion? The "gouffre" of death, let us remember, is to Baudelaire both space and time: statues seem to him *divine*.

In *Les Fleurs du Mal*, Baudelaire's dandyism has its feminine counterpart. He does not extol his languorous tropical natives nearly as much as the stylized deities who torment and charm him: "statue with jet eyes, bronze-browed angel," he says to one of them, showing the link between spirituality and pure matter. His metaphors mine inorganic nature for symbols of sterility and frigidity: metals and minerals that are hard and cold. It would be wrong to interpret these images as Parnassian conventions. They are the active agents of the denaturalization of woman. They effect a metamorphosis. Sonnet 27 lets us see, line by line, this progressive, Ovidian, incantatory petrification of a woman's lithe body, until in the last alexandrine shines, like a star, "the cold majesty of the sterile woman." In a large group of poems dealing with natural woman in "ascetic terms," the sonnet to Beauty occupies a central position. Rather than a neo-classic ideal, it enacts the intellectual *askesis* of Baudelaire's life:

> Je suis belle, ô mortels! comme un rêve de pierre,
> Et mon sein, où chacun s'est meurtri tour à tour,
> Est fait pour inspirer au poète un amour
> Eternel et muet ainsi que la matière.[38]

Here, the metallic shell of dandyism becomes shaped into the artist's dream, a *plenum*, no longer a protection against nature, but a new, completely *artistic* state of being. Rather

---

[38] Baudelaire, *Œuvres complètes*, "La Beauté," p. 96.

WALLACE STEVENS
and the Symbolist Imagination

than a neo-classicist, this love of petrified life makes Baudelaire a precursor of the Surrealists, those innocence-seekers for whom "the way to purity is through mineralization."
Michel Carrouges, in *La Mystique du Surhomme*, quotes this revealing dream of Baudelaire:

> ". . . j'étais un morceau de glace pensant, je me considérais comme une statue taillée dans un seul bloc de glace; et cette folle hallucination me causait une fierté, excitait en moi un bien-être moral que je ne saurais définir."[39]

This mystique of cold and insensitivity comes directly out of Baudelaire's wish to purify nature, for the Dandy's beauty "consiste surtout dans l'air *froid* qui vient de l'inébranlable résolution de ne pas être ému."[40] But his "cold" and his "freezing" is not the result of naturally cold mountain air, as it is in Nietzsche or Stevens. It is a petrification and a congealing of life wrought by a desire for a contracted, homogeneous, absolute purity. It is the reverse of the Nietzschean or the Stevensian expansion from an imaginary mountain-top. In Baudelaire's statue of ice we cannot recognize the prototype of Stevens' familiar "man of glass, / Who in a million diamonds sums us up."[41] The genesis of Baudelaire's purity is a progressive decreation: clothes to hide animality, make-up to hide time, jewels to replace flesh, and the final petrification and divinization. Baudelaire's man of ice is the result of a centripetal movement, toward nothing-

---

[39] Baudelaire, *Œuvres complètes*, pp. 93-97.
[40] Baudelaire, *Œuvres complètes*, p. 909.
[41] *C.P.*, p. 250.

ness, but this new creation he reaches is the product of art: clothes-in-depth. Stevens' man of ice lives in change, and is nudity-in-depth.

If, indeed, Stevens took up dandyism as a profession, this must be understood as a gesture of self-protection, not self-purification and *askesis*. It would be wrong to call it "a dandyism of contentment" any longer. Yet the clothing metaphors in *Harmonium* belong to a universe of colors and shapes as imaginative safeguards. Its aesthetics are the Baudelairian "correspondances" between nature and man, not the opposite Baudelairian exclusion of nature. And when eventually, after a silence of six years, the *askesis* of *Ideas of Order* appears, it will seek purity in an Adamic innocence, not an artistic petrification.

Stevens and Mallarmé

> He wanted to see. He wanted the eye to see
> And not be touched by blue. He wanted to know,
> A naked man who regarded himself in the glass
> Of air, who looked for the world beneath the blue,
> Without blue, without any turquoise tint or phase,
> Any azure under-side or after-color. . . .[42]

Among the poetic notions linking Stevens to Mallarmé, that of "purity" fosters the most satisfying impression of a resemblance between the two poets. Did not Stevens admonish himself to "seek those purposes that are purely purposes of the pure poet . . ."? The same entry in *Adagia* defines "purity" almost in the terms of Poe's *The Poetic*

[42] C.P., p. 241.

Principle, thus seeming to close the loop of tradition spiraling from Poe to Mallarmé, Valéry, and Abbé Brémond:

> To give a sense of the freshness or vividness of life is a valid purpose for poetry. A didactic purpose justifies itself in the mind of the teacher; a philosophical purpose justifies itself in the mind of the philosopher. It is not that one purpose is as justifiable as another but that some purposes are pure, others impure.[43]

Wallace Stevens' "sense of the freshness or vividness of life" is a snug fit to Poe's "Poetic Sentiment": "He recognizes [it] . . . in the volutes of the flower—in the clustering of low shrubberies—in the waving of the grain-fields—in the slanting of tall, Eastern trees—in the blue distance of mountains—in the grouping of clouds. . . ."[44] This clearly based Poe's angelism on earth. Somehow, Stevens repatriated the angel to the American soil, and restored the original meaning of "pure poetry": "In spite of M. Brémond, pure poetry is a term that has grown to be descriptive of poetry in which not the true subject but the poetry of the subject is paramount."[45] The difference between Stevens and the French tradition hinges on the metaphysical meaning of the word *pure.* It is a contrast between feeling purity in the world, and reaching purity out of this world by an angel's flight.

Mallarmé's distortion of Poe ("giving a purer meaning to his nation's words") takes the form of an angel wielding a naked sword: he is the angel of death, whose symbol of purification and severance typifies Mallarmé's imagination

[43] *O.P.,* p. 157. [44] Edgar A. Poe, *The Poetic Principle.*
[45] *P.O.,* p. 222.

rather than Poe's. It is an imagination of dualistic structures, of earth and sky as enemies, "du sol et de la nue hostiles," of light and darkness, of antithesis, of the monster and the hero fighting.[46] Stevens insists, on the contrary, that *his* angel has "neither ashen wing nor wear of ore" and is one of the countrymen:

> I am one of you and being one of you
> Is being and knowing what I am and know.
>
> Yet I am the necessary angel of earth,
> Since, in my sight, you see the earth again,
>
> Cleared of its stiff and stubborn, man-locked set . . . .[47]

The genesis of this image (a picture by Tal Coat representing a Venetian glass and earthenware round it) associates "Angel Surrounded by Paysans" with all the other poems by Stevens in which the poetic act is symbolized by a metamorphosis into glass, and in which purity is the result of cleared sight.

Mallarmé, whose poetry Stevens read at least as early as 1914, may have originated the meaning of "pure" as ideally transparent and visible. It is a key-word, occurring no fewer than seventeen times in a small body of poetry. However, several other notions are mixed with that of sheer visibility, for instance in

Le pur vase d'aucun breuvage.[48]

[46] Stéphane Mallarmé, "Le Tombeau d'Edgar Poe," *Œuvres complètes*, Paris, 1945, p. 70.

[47] C.P., pp. 496-97.

[48] Mallarmé, *Œuvres complètes*, p. 74.

WALLACE STEVENS
and the Symbolist Imagination

It is absence made visible. Purity will have to shed its Mal-
larméan connotations of inaccessibility and non-being before
finding its way into Stevens' imaginary world. Yet the rela-
tionship of *pure* poetry unites the two poets, at least in dis-
similitude.

They shared a revealing enthusiasm for the Impressionists.
Mallarmé called their art "clairvoyance," "abstract purifica-
tion into the beautiful," and "the modern enchantment."[49]
Of Manet's eye, he said that it was "virgin and abstract."[50]
Purity, then, has its origin deep in the artist's sight, not in
the world. Its brilliance is an emanation of the artist's eye:

> Le Maître, par un œil profond, a sur ses pas,
> Apaisé de l'éden l'inquiète merveille
> . . . pluie ou diamant, le regard diaphane
> Resté là sur ces fleurs dont nulle ne se fane.[51]

The Master is not a painter but a poet, Théophile Gautier,
whose ever-freshening gaze stops the decay of flowers.
Poetry and painting reach purity. But the metamorphosis
is a swift passage from sheer visibility ("regard diaphane")
to essential notion. The slow, Ovidian metamorphosis be-
longs to the imagination of the vessel: the metaphor as shell.
Mallarmé's is the metaphor as fold. An earthly flower be-
comes a "pure" flower, "absente de tous bouquets" by an
ontological jump into abstraction. No doubt that Mallarmé's
definition of poetry as the "Orphic explication of the earth"
calls upon the poet to *unfold* flatly a world distanced from

---

[49] Mallarmé, *Œuvres complétes*, p. 536.
[50] Mallarmé, *Œuvres complètes*, p. 532.
[51] Mallarmé, *Œuvres complètes*, p. 55.

the visible one by negative analogy. The transaction between
the eye and reality is a "transposition":

> A quoi bon la merveille de transposer un fait de nature en
> sa presque disparition vibratoire selon le jeu de la parole,
> cependant, si ce n'est qu'en émane, sans la gêne d'un
> proche ou concret rappel, la notion pure.[52]

A symbol duplicates a "fact" in the mind; abstract, it is
"pure." An imagination such as Mallarmé's will not create
a paradise of calm sensual presences, beautiful shapes and
colors; it will decreate appearances, bring death to forestall
death, thus master death, and save from decay a "pure"
world in the mind:

> Oui, dans une île que l'air charge
> De vue et non de visions
> Toute fleur s'étalait plus large
> Sans que nous en devisions.
>
> Telles, immenses, que chacune
> Ordinairement se para
> D'un lucide contour, lacune,
> Qui des jardins la separa.
>
> Gloire du long désir, Idées . . . .[53]

Stevens, who quoted the last line while prefacing a Valéryan
dialogue, could not have recognized this paradise as native
ground. For Mallarmé's paradise of perception is a mental
island outside nature. A clear outline separates it from

[52] Mallarmé, *Œuvres complètes*, p. 857.
[53] Mallarmé, *Œuvres complètes*, p. 56.

earthly gardens. Purity means schism. Divorce, not marriage, is the law of the poet's hygienic vision.

To Stevens, on the contrary, transparence brought participation. His comments on the Impressionists bespoke his delight that their art removed a barrier between him and nature. The main notion conveyed, sixteen times out of nineteen occurrences, by his use of the word "pure," is a cleansing of the verbal medium. Reality *is* pure. The Adamic tradition does not accept the sense of a Fall. Then purity results from clearing sight of its "man-locked set" of religious ideas and mythological metaphors. The object is not made pure by the artist's eye, it is cleansed by it, until "The poem refreshes life so that we share, / For a moment, the first idea. . . ."[54] The terms in which Stevens speaks of pure reality are unequivocally the language of romantic participation. His "first idea" is not at all Mallarmé's Platonic *Idée*. He explained it in terms of pictorial visibility:

> Someone here wrote me the other day and wanted to know what I meant by a thinker of the first idea. If you take the varnish and dirt of generations off a picture, you see it in its first idea. If you think about the world without its varnish and dirt, you are a thinker of the first idea.[55]

The linguistic equivalent of such a cleaning-up (which, incidentally, makes man a god)[56] takes place in many poems in which Stevens, instead of Poe, gives a "purer" meaning to

[54] *C.P.*, p. 382.
[55] Letter to Henry Church, October 28, 1942.
[56] See Pearce, *The Continuity of American Poetry*, p. 419.

his nation's words; most clearly in "A Primitive like an Orb," where the words for tree and cloud and sky "lose the old uses" that men made of them. Would not the poet luxuriate in the joy of a pure language: a language whose words might readily take the place of things, like the painter's brush strokes? He would then become as "clairvoyant" as an Impressionist, since his medium would lose its opacity, and he could release "Free knowledges, secreted until then."[57]

Both Stevens and Mallarmé wanted a necessary relation between words and things. But they differed in their way of coming to terms with the inescapable arbitrariness of language. In accord with his aesthetics of separation, Mallarmé sought to purify by cutting. He broke each word away from its wonted associations. Hence the fragmented sentence, in which each word, gemlike and pure, reflects the next unearthed jewel. Almost nothing of this divisive technique in Stevens' style: metaphors seem to generate one another instead of being juxtaposed forcibly by *folding* one word on top of another. Another contrast is vocabulary: while Mallarmé purified by sterilizing (two thousand different words in all), Stevens freshened by renewing (most words are used only once or twice in any collection of his poems into books). Note how exact Stevens' terminology was when he said "the poem refreshes life"—not the world, "so that we share the first idea"—not pure "azur." Since all we want is a new *sense* of things, renewing the words will do. The Impressionist impulse goes toward the transparence of the medium, and eschews the issue of absolutes. Stevens

[57] *C.P.*, p. 441.

takes "pure poetry" to mean poetry written "because one grows tired . . . of one's imagination."[58] Or in another wording: "Poetry constantly requires a new relation."[59]

Even more than Mallarmé, Stevens is the poet of nakedness. By "more" is meant both quality and quantity. Relatively to the prose of his time, Mallarmé's high proportion (*nu* and *nudité* used twenty times) defines "nu" as a keyword.[60] Terms like "bare," "bareness," "nude," "nudity," "naked," "nakedness" recur in all ninety times in Stevens' *Collected Poems* alone. More significant are the imaginary structures that actually make these words "key-words" and that differentiate Stevens' poetic world from Mallarmé's.

Mallarmé's imaginary space, that is the space generated by his imagery in the reader's mind, is characterized by partitions, dividing surfaces, which are at the same time transparent and forbidding. One of these images recurs with connotations of beauty and death: it is the mirror. It reveals nakedness but also locks it out of reach:

> Elle, défunte nue en le miroir, encor
> Que, dans l'oubli fermé par le cadre, se fixe
> De scintillations sitôt le septuor.[61]

Charles Mauron psychoanalyzed this image of the poet's dead sister or mother, as a source of guilt and desire. Not only the mirror, but the cenotaph slab is imagined as translucid and as a means of keeping a distance between the self and the naked body. But whether or not the Freudians are

---

[58] *O.P.*, p. 221.   [59] *O.P.*, p. 178.
[60] P. Guiraud, *Index du Vocabulaire du Symbolisme*, III, Paris, 1953.
[61] Mallarmé, *Œuvres complètes*, p. 69.

right, whether or not they can add a third dead woman to
Mallarmé's private morgue,[62] does not matter to us as read-
ers, although Stevens was aware of Mauron's theory. What
matters is the impossibility of crossing the dividing surface,
or the punishment which attends its crossing. Mallarmé
conceived this act as his aesthetic and metaphysical achieve-
ment: "It is now two years since I committed the sin of
seeing the Dream in its ideal nakedness, whilst I ought to
have heaped between it and me a mystery of music and
forgetting,"[63] he writes to a friend while at work on *Hérodi-
ade*. Direct sight of nakedness is to Mallarmé both a goal
and a taboo.

Mallarmé cogently placed nakedness on the other side of
a partition which the poetic act must penetrate. Nakedness
is akin to a metaphysical rebirth. The terms "naïf" or "natif"
associate with nudity. But it is an impossible rebirth. The
most misunderstood instance of this theme is perhaps "Le
Pitre Châtié." We must ignore the early version produced
by Dr. Bonniot, and which may indeed address Marie Ger-
hard's eyes. The new poem introduces the theme of "Les
Fenêtres," the break-through:

> J'ai troué dans le mur de toile une fenêtre.
>
> .   .   .   .   .   .
>
> Tout à coup le soleil frappe la nudité
> Qui pure s'exhala de ma fraîcheur de nacre.[64]

---

[62] Cf. L. Cellier, *Mallarmé et la Morte Qui Parle*, Paris, 1959.

[63] Cited by R. Champigny, "Mallarmé's Relation to Platonism and
Romanticism," *Modern Language Review*, LI (July, 1956), p. 356.

[64] Mallarmé, *Œuvres complètes*, p. 31.

WALLACE STEVENS
and the Symbolist Imagination

Once through the wall, the clown falls, finds both purification and a "thousand tombs," innocence and the dead sister (Ophelia, objectifying the good Hamlet),[65] but the forbidden water of the lake-mirror dissolves the film of make-up which was his "whole art." His skin has lost the purity of youthful innocence, and its nudity is left exposed to the sun's punishment. The 1884 version of "Le Pitre Châtié" tells almost the reverse of the first version: not that the love of a woman distracts the artist from his art, but that the quest for an ideal nakedness has failed. The attempt to replace the relationship with words (which are, like soot, a grimy make-up of ideality) by a relationship of naked, undistanced, unmediated vision, was an ontological impossibility. With this poem, the polarity of the veiled and the naked completes a striking image of the Symbolist poet. Qua *littérateur*, he praises make-up.[66] But qua poetic hero, he yearns for a virginal nudity, with its imagery of frozen lakes and immobilized swans bringing him death and sterility. Indeed, we can see how the nakedness of the poet, symbolizing

[65] "Reniant le Mauvais Hamlet" should be construed with reference to Mallarmé's notion that Hamlet was in fact divided into a bad Hamlet and a good one impersonated by Ophelia, "the virgin objectified youth of the lamentable royal heir." Mallarmé, "Hamlet," *Œuvres complètes*, p. 302.

[66] He even sells it in his fashion magazine, *La Dernière Mode*. As the promoter of cold cream, Mallarmé is the subject of a brilliant analysis by J.-P. Richard, *L'Univers Imaginaire de Mallarmé*, Paris, 1961, pp. 91-93. Also cf. this telling passage, "Je lisais donc un de ces chers poèmes (dont les plaques de fard ont plus de charme pour moi que l'incarnat de la jeunesse)." Mallarmé, *Divagations*, Paris, p. 24.

linguistic *askesis,* is a strange and terrible metaphor. It makes aesthetics similar to a glacier both transparent and denying transparence to the poet it will eventually paralyze.

There is a third image: the poet as *voyeur.* J.-P. Richard shows its relevance. For beside cold nudity, Mallarmé knows summer desire. Beside the Virgin Muse live the nymphs of "L'Après-midi d'un Faune" and the heroines of *Contes Indiens.* Stevens (whose Harvard friend Walter Arensberg translated "L'Après-midi d'un Faune" in his book *Idols*) was at first more attentive to nudity as such than as aesthetic symbol. Indeed the Voyant-Voyeur relationship links Stevens with Mallarmé. One cannot read "Apostrophe to Vincentine" without recalling the beautiful vowel and color contrasts of Hérodiade's "native unveiling" ("De mes robes, arôme aux farouches délices / Sortirait le frisson blanc de ma nudité"),[67] and W. Y. Tindall rightly affiliates "The Virgin Carrying a Lantern" to "Une Négresse par le Démon Secouée."[68] Other poems in the voyeuristic manner of Mallarmé are "Cy Est Pourtraicte, Madame Ste Ursule, et Les Unze Mille Vierges" and of course "Peter Quince at the Clavier."

If *Harmonium* is largely a book of nudes and beautiful barenesses, *Ideas of Order* the book of a bare, unpoetic reality, *Parts of a World* can be called the book of heroic nakedness. The distribution of the terms "nude," "bare," and "naked"—a distinction unavailable in French—grows with

[67] Mallarmé, *Œuvres complètes,* p. 47.
[68] *Wallace Stevens,* p. 18.

the use of the words "abstraction," "purity," and "nothing-ness."

	Nude	Bare	Naked	Pure	Noth-ing-ness	Abstrac-tion
Harmonium	5	10	8	3	2	0
Ideas of Order	2	7	3	0	4	0
Blue Guitar	0	1	1	0	0	2
Owl's Clover	0	1	0	0	0	0
Parts of a World	1	2	16	5	1	6
Transport to Summer	2	5	9	7	6	8
Auroras of Autumn	0	7	8	4	6	4
The Rock	0	0	2	0	2	1[69]

The statistics of this development show that the influence of Mallarmé came late; that without doubt the habit of using the words "naked" and "nakedness" with their crucial aesthetic or epistemological meanings parallels the Mallarméan practice. What statistics do not show is that Stevens' definition of nakedness contradicts the French "nudité." Stevens' bare jar, "like nothing else in Tennessee," bore even less resemblance (except as poetic artifact) to Mallarmé's "pur vase d'aucun breuvage."

The fourth section of "Peter Quince at the Clavier" al-

[69] Nude and nudity, bare, bareness, and barenesses, naked and naked-ness, pure and purity, abstract and abstraction were lumped together.

Grateful acknowledgments are hereby given to Professor Thomas Kurtz and Mr. Thomas Martin, of the Dartmouth Computing Center, and to the Research Committee of Dartmouth College for making this word-count possible.

The high proportion of words denoting nakedness (90 in all out of a total of about 83,000 words) is to be noticed relatively to the absence of these words in Dewey's 1923 count of 100,000 words. This differential is what makes them key-words according to Guiraud's definition (in *Index du Vocabulaire du Symbolisme*, III).

ready implies that the peeping Tom's perception of beauty was incomplete:

> Beauty is momentary in the mind—
> The fitful tracing of a portal;
> But in the flesh it is immortal.

This is Impressionism triumphant. Appearance is all. The elders' *red* eyes see through their desire, in the mind. This kind of music will escape, fitful, momentary, because it is a subjective feeling ("music is feeling . . . not sound").[70] Permanent beauty is not a Mallarméan or Neoplatonic Idea, but the revelation of an actual presence among us, on earth. In the teeth of Platonism and docetism, Stevens affirms what Robert Pack and Amos Wilder call the mystery of incarnation. The essence of things depends on their perishable existence. Such appears to be the difficult, modern, meaning of Susanna's legend. Stevens insists on nudity as essence revealed by existence:

NUDITY AT THE CAPITAL

> But nakedness, woolen massa, concerns an innermost atom.
> If that remains concealed, what does the bottom matter?

This defines nakedness as a quality at the center (the capital) of being, and not as something on the other side of a glass wall, like Mallarmé's "nudité idéale."

Nakedness at the center: the image links Stevens' private goemetry with his mode of perception. It is a recurrent image, a key-image, important for the understanding of

[70] C.P., p. 90.

WALLACE STEVENS
and the Symbolist Imagination

Ideas of Order, "The Man with the Blue Guitar," and *Parts of a World.* The search for centrality and for nakedness is a single movement, the ascensional movement of a human hero. Stevens' symbols have extraordinary power because of their very ordinariness: blue air, the mountaintop, the giant, the circle, and the center. Majesty, clairvoyance, and nakedness coalesce. What we might call "Hoon's complex" unifies the "high imagination" in which Stevens now sings triumphantly.

It is an old atomistic imagining that looking is actually like breathing, one that Lucretius accredited by calling things thus seen "spirantia." The transaction between the eye and the center of nakedness, by an odd parallel, often strikes Stevens as an exchange like breath:

> And *naked* of any illusion, in poverty,
> In the exactest poverty, if then
> One *breathed* the cold evening, the deepest inhalation
> Would come from that return to the subtle centre.[71]

This synesthesia makes the reader more conscious of the Romantic "communion" of the eye, Stevens' phrase in the same poem. It is, as an image, worth ten pages of aesthetic theory. For instance, it rejects Mallarmé's asceticism, much as Rémy de Gourmont did.[72] Purity is not something reach-

[71] *C.P.*, p. 258.

[72] See Glen S. Burne's excellent summary of post-Mallarméan aesthetics, *Rémy de Gourmont* (Carbondale, Ill., 1963); "Indeed, Gourmont reversed the order of causality established by other Symbolists and asserted that it is not the will which places the artist in the center of a network of stimuli . . . sensation is the principal condition of creation," p. 49.

ing out of the artist's eye at will. It is breathed in. Perception is participation, an organic relationship between the circle of appearances and the center of the self:

> . . . Breathe, breathe upon the centre of
> The breath life's latest, thousand senses.
> But let this one sense be the single main.[73]

Stevens' poetry is central in the sense that Nietzsche's poetry is central, that is, centered on the self. Its climate differs from the Symbolist descent into a dark room. It is real air, breathed on an imaginary or real mountain: a Mount Penn, or a Mount Chocorua, or a Mountain in Vermont,[74] or even Nietzsche's Alps.[75] The air breathed at the top gives all its values to the hero. It makes him purer, larger, more central. In fact the *air makes* the hero, thus dilated to the limits of the universe, and at the same time concentrated:

> He was a shell of dark blue glass, or ice,
> Or air collected in a deep essay,
>
> . . . . . .
>
> Upon my top he breathed the pointed dark.
>
> . . . . . .
>
> The air changes, creates, and re-creates, like strength,

[73] C.P., p. 264.
[74] See "Late Hymn from the Myrrh-Mountain," C.P., p. 349.
   "Chocorua to its Neighbor," C.P., p. 296.
   "The Man with the Blue Guitar," C.P., p. 176.
   "Three Travelers Watch a Sunrise," O.P., p. 127.
   "July Mountain," O.P., p. 114.
[75] "The pensive man. . . . He sees that eagle float
   For which the intricate Alps are a single nest." C.P., p. 216.

WALLACE STEVENS
and the Symbolist Imagination

> And to breathe is a fulfilling of desire,
> A clearing, a detecting, a completing,
> A largeness lived and not conceived, a space
> That is an instant nature, brilliantly.[76]

As poet of air, Stevens differs from Baudelaire and Mallarmé. Their dream of metamorphosis into a "glorious body" seeks an escape from cosmic law. Baudelaire stops at petrification; Mallarmé conquers the freedom of nothingness beyond "L'insensibilité de l'azur et des pierres."[77] Because of a basic coalition of sight, breath, and touch in his perception, Stevens imagines his metamorphosis into a non-body as an increase of body-senses:

> To change nature, not merely to change ideas,
> To escape from the body, so to feel
> Those feelings that the body balks,
> The feelings of the natures round us here:
> As a boat feels when it cuts blue water.[78]

The joy of the hero is that sensual nakedness of the keel, that contact with elements, that immediate feel of reality touched, seen, breathed in like air or like water, "instant nature," brilliant, cleared, "lived and not conceived." It is the joy of being both on the horizon of the multiplied aspects of reality and at the naked center. Or rather, nakedness is that quality of the object and of man which abolishes the irradiating distance between the circle and the center.

"The natures round us here": this alone establishes

---

[76] *C.P.*, pp. 297-301.   [77] "Tristesse d'Été."   [78] *C.P.*, p. 234.

Stevens' originality. His movement from plural to singular goes from circle to center. And this figure is not the critic's device, but a structure of Stevens' imagination as well as a constant tenet of his aesthetics. From Crispin's idea that his soil is man's intelligence, to the notion that the "central man," the man of glass, "is the transparence of the place in which / He is,"[79] it is evident that the centripetal structure develops. In contrast, the centrifugal moments are few: perhaps the concentric domination of man spreading a perimeter of order in the chaos of forms ("Anecdote of the Jar") or the mastery of song fixing zones and poles of light ("Idea of Order at Key West"), or the mad captain's take-over of the world by an ever-widening circle of the will ("Life on a Battleship"). Stevens' preferred figure of transcendence, on the contrary, is in the wording of the last poem, "to be / Merely the center of a circle." The restrictive adverb means, in its context, that man must return to the earth stripped of its myths, to the earth of "Sunday Morning." The centripetal imagination of Stevens moves toward a pure center where it will find peace.

What is that center: a man of glass, an essential poem, a giant of nothingness, a supreme fiction? The multiplicity of names might suggest divinity! And an unpublished letter from the poet to the keen critic of his metamorphoses might strengthen that impression:

> . . . I do not want to turn to stone under your very eyes by saying "This is the centre that I seek and this alone."

[79] C.P., p. 250.

WALLACE STEVENS
and the Symbolist Imagination

> Your mind is too much like my own for it to seem an evasion on my part to say merely that I do seek a centre and expect to go on seeking it. I don't say that I shall not find it as that I do not expect to find it. It is the great necessity even without specific identification.[80]

This program for poetry differs from a mysticism. It is the quest not for a god, but for a man; not for an ideal perfection, but for reality. It also differs from Baudelaire's attempted identification with the infinite sphere and the infinite center of the Divinity, from his "vaporisation et concentration du moi." It differs again from Mallarmé's immobilization at the center of a circle of nothingness.[81] The metaphors of concealment and divestment help us to understand Stevens' difficulty: that center which he seeks is both reality and a self. It tends to naked reality through a centripetal movement. For things reveal their essence as a sum of profiles. Stevens' ascetic look resembles the phenomenologist's *epoché* much more than it does the Symbolist's *askesis*:

>   ... We seek
> The poem of pure reality, untouched
> By trope or deviation, straight to the word,
> Straight to the transfixing object, to the object
>
> At the exactest point at which it is itself,
> Transfixing by being purely what it is,
> A view of New Haven, say, through a certain eye,

[80] Letter to Sister Bernetta Quinn, April 7, 1949.
[81] Cf. Poulet, *Les Métamorphoses du Cercle*, Paris, 1961, p. 449.

> The eye made clear of uncertainty, with the sight
> Of simple seeing, without reflection. We seek
> Nothing beyond reality. Within it,
>
> Everything . . . .[82]

The "transfixing object" is a residue, at a "center of resemblance," like the pineapple "reduced" from the "sum of its complications": it is an image of convergence to a center.[83] Our imperfections, as Stevens calls our successive views of reality (Husserl's *Abschattungen*) form a circle of shapes, colors, metaphors. Keeping this world on the move will guarantee the fixity of its center: "It Must Change," so that the perceptive self may be evolved. The pure object reveals the pure self, or should; the naked thing mirrors a naked man, or should. Such are the abstract terms of the exchange. Stevens' poetry produces poems like "An Ordinary Evening in New Haven" out of a faith: the faith that the imagination can or should try to apprehend reality, and in so doing, apprehends itself. This view, offered as conclusion, can serve to distinguish on one side the dualistic imagination of Mallarmé and Valéry, issuing the same hyperbolic doubt of reality as Descartes' Cogito, and on the other side the Romantic imagination culminating in Husserl's Cogito:

> The flux of living, my flux, as thinking subject, can be largely unapprehended, unknown to any extent of its past or future, it is enough to look at life in flux and actually present, for me to say, without any restriction and of

[82] C.P., p. 471.
[83] N.A., pp. 83-89.

WALLACE STEVENS
and the Symbolist Imagination

necessity: *I am*, this life is, I live: *cogito*.[84] But Stevens'
final yes, born of a transparence turned to philosophic
glass, was already present in the imaginative matrix of
Harmonium.

[1961, 1964]

[84] Edmund Husserl, *Ideen zu einer reinen Phänomenologie und
phänomenologischen Philosophie*, I, The Hague, 1950, p. 85. That
Stevens was attracted to phenomenology is quite certain. In a "Collect
of Philosophy" O.P., p. 194, he mentions a letter from Jean Wahl
about Husserl's *Méditations Cartésiennes*, about Pascal's image of the
infinite sphere, and finally about Traherne's poetry. Incidentally, Tra-
herne's circular imagery was treated in an article of *Études Anglaises*,
Vol. 14-2 (April-June 1961), by Jean Wahl.

4
Apollinaire

From this I shall evolve a man

("The Man with the Blue Guitar")

THERE IS NO massive evidence to link Wallace Stevens with Guillaume Apollinaire. But this is perhaps to the good. Massive evidence of one poet's influence on another must be handled gingerly. It might kill two bards with one stone. Indeed, conscious influence functions the same way as conscious intention does. If there is no meaning in a poem beyond what the author meant it to mean, as soon as its inspiring influence has been exposed all its meaning vanishes. For a long time, comparative literature resembled the positivistic science of iconography. Now, Erwin Panofsky showed what was wrong with iconography. It mutilated meaning by considering only a part of meaning: themes, images, myths. Iconology, as opposed by Panofsky to iconography, apprehends the intrinsic meaning of a work of art by treating its composition, its themes, and even its materials "as symptoms of 'symbolical values' which are often unknown to the artist himself and may even emphatically differ from what he intended to express."[1] Iconology is a structural science. "It corrects the interpretation of an individual work of art by a 'history of style' which in turn can only be built up by interpreting individual works."[2] Such is the methodological circle which we must accept if we forego massive evidence, and try to prove the truth of a parallelism by the truths which it permits us to discover.

How do we know, then, that Stevens and Apollinaire

[1] Erwin Panofsky, "Iconography and Iconology," in *Meaning in the Visual Arts*, New York, 1955, pp. 26-39.

[2] Panofsky, *Meaning in the Visual Arts*. For a brilliant discussion of Panofsky's method as a structuralist, see Pierre Bourdieu's Postface to his translation of Panofsky's *Architecture et pensée scholastique*, Paris, 1967, pp. 135-167.

WALLACE STEVENS
and the Symbolist Imagination

should be compared? We perceive at once what separates
them. It is only through an effort of abstraction that we can
see what unifies them. First we must abstract their poetic
careers. Although they were born just one year apart, Stevens
in 1879 and Apollinaire in 1880, one could hardly call
them contemporaries. By 1918, when Apollinaire died, Ste-
vens had but a handful of poems in little magazines. Only
near his death, in 1955, did he become, like Apollinaire, a
culture hero. Yet, in spite of all the differences between the
young Turk and the late bloomer, one a penniless journalist
and the other an executive mammonite, a striking parallelism
exists in their poetic development. The stylistic transforma-
tions which occurred between 1910 and 1912 in Apollinaire's
poetry and between 1930 and 1937 in Stevens' were charac-
terized in both by a crisis of their Symbolist values, and
caused in part by a great deal of thinking about cubist
painting. The basis for our comparison is simply that the
same painters seem to have served Stevens as well as Apolli-
naire in their progress toward a style of modernism.

We should refrain, however, from fancying Stevens as
some Manhattan counterpart of Apollinaire among the
Montmartre painters. Two years after the Armory Show,
Stevens wrote to his wife:

Dear Bud: Walter Arensberg telephoned yesterday after-
noon and asked me to take dinner with him at the Bre-
voort with Marcel Duchamp, the man who painted *The
Nude Descending a Staircase*. . . . After dinner we went
up to Arensberg's apartment and looked at some of Du-
champ's things. I made very little of them. But naturally,

without sophistication in that direction and with only a very rudimentary feeling about art, I expect little of myself (*L.W.S.* 185).

Yet from such modest beginnings Stevens went on to be "the ultimate Plato with Picasso's guitar" as Delmore Schwartz dubbed him.[3] He was to be the art man whose perspective transformed American poetry because art had transformed his perspective as an artist and as a man. We see the first symptoms of this change in the poems of *Ideas of Order* (1935), but the best proofs are to be found in *The Man with the Blue Guitar* (1937), whose style breaks quite clear from previous collections. Besides the title, it contains several allusions to Cézanne and Picasso. In addition, we now have a letter dated March 17, 1937, which completes the impression made by the poems:

> Dear Mr. Latimer: During the winter I have written something like 35 or 40 short pieces of which about 25 seem to be coming through. They deal with the relation or balance between imagined things and real things which, as you know, is a constant source of trouble to me. . . . Perhaps it would be better to say that what they deal with is the painter's problem of realization (*L.W.S.* 316).

We must abstract again. By "realization" Stevens seems to mean the metamorphosis of real things into another reality. *Real things* has two meanings, natural reality and, since North America has no "ruins" worthy of the name, modern reality. Our first parallel between Apollinaire and Stevens

[3] *The Harvard Advocate*, cxxvii (December 1940), p. 11.

WALLACE STEVENS
and the Symbolist Imagination

will explore these relations, with constant recourse to the example of painting as the *tiers commun* that unites the two poets.

It would be quite wrong to say that Apollinaire introduced modern reality into his poems only after his contact with Cubism; in fact the reverse has a chance of being true. But Duchamp, Léger, Delaunay, and of course Braque and Picasso showed him how to cope with the modern in its own right, with its own style. Impressionism had secularized the subject matter of painting. But consider the picture of the St. Lazare station by Monet. The steel rafters, the smoke are painted with the same technique as are trees and river mists. The modern object is swallowed up in the great thematic viscosity of the picture, and fragmented into a multitude of contrasted signs. It is digested. Naturalized. Here is such a landscape from the group of Rhineland poems. *Les Rhénanes*:

> Sur la route bordant le fleuve et tachée d'ombre
>   Fuyaient tremblant de peur
> Comme des chevaliers indignes les autos
> Tandis qu'au fil du Rhin s'en allaient les bateaux
>   A vapeur.   (*o.p.* 351)[4]

Against the slow natural rhythm of the river, Apollinaire plays up the speed of cars and boats. But why the craven knight analogy, if not to integrate by it what seemed pejorative to Symbolist values? We verify the same attitude,

---

[4] For Apollinaire's work we follow this code:

o.p.—*Oeuvres Poétiques*, Bibliothèque de la Pléiade, Paris, 1956.

c.p.—*The Cubist Painters*, translated by Lionel Abel, Wittenborn, 1944.

this time toward urban modernity, in a night scene from
La Chanson du mal-aimé:

> Soirs de Paris ivres du gin
> Flambant de l'électricité
> Les tramways feux verts sur l'échine
> Musiquent au long des portées
> De rails leur folie de machines. (*o.p.* 59)

Roger Shattuck writes: "It is the prosody here that transforms the shoddiness of modern life into something both
moving and comic."[5] Essentially, modernity is redeemed, as
in the first example, by funny enjambments, tricky neologisms, and by being included in poetic conventions, whether
of symbol or of form.

After his initiation to Cubism, Apollinaire no longer felt
the need to apologize for machines. He adopted modern
reality with the same enthusiasm as did his friend Delaunay,
the painter of Eiffel towers, whose pure colors and idealized
shapes impressed the poet of "Zone":

J'ai vu ce matin une jolie rue dont j'ai oublié le nom
Neuve et propre du soleil elle était le clairon
Les directeurs les ouvriers et les belles sténo-dactylographes
Du lundi matin au samedi soir quatre fois par jour y passent . . . .
J'aime la grâce de cette rue industrielle
Située entre la rue Aumont-Thiéville et la place des Ternes.

(o.p. 39-40)

A new rhythm here hurries to the pace of modernity. It is
achieved by cramming five or six syllables into measures that
had room for three or four at the most. A word like *sténo-*

---

[5] Roger Shattuck, *The Banquet Years*, New York, 1961, p. 318.

WALLACE STEVENS
and the Symbolist Imagination

dactylographes fits no traditional mold. It is a fragile material, akin to the flimsy fabrications in Picasso's *papiers collés*. Not only is the machine age represented, it furnishes the means of its representation.[6]

The new awareness of space was symbolized by the radio station atop the Eiffel Tower. On his first painting of the Tower in 1909, Delaunay had written that the Tower addresses the whole world.[7] This was the starting point for simultanism, which was simultaneously invented by Cendrars and Apollinaire. Its techniques, varying from ubiquity in space to a perspectival dance round the object, stem from a psychological principle that seemed much more realistic than one-point perspective and sequential development. Bergson had called it the simultaneity of states of consciousness. That it was revealed to the poets by the painters only verifies the validity of approaching their style through painting.

If we now compare Stevens' realization of modern reality with Apollinaire's, we start with rather meagre iconographical booty. In *Harmonium*, almost nothing. The "thin men of Haddam" (*C.P.* 93) and the mysterious "firecats" of Oklahoma which probably were oil wells, give practically the only clues to industrial North America. Stevens was then, and remained almost successfully in spite of encroaching

[6] For the emphasis placed on the relationship between Cubism and the machine age, I am indebted to a very good book by Pierre Francastel, *Art et technique*, Paris, 1956, especially pp. 166-79.

[7] Cited by Francastel in Delaunay, *Du Cubisme à l'art abstrait*, SEVPEN, Paris, 1967, p. 21. The whole inscription reads: "Exposition universelle 1889, la Tour à l'univers s'adresse . . . mouvement et profondeur, 1909 France-Russie."

urbanization or because of it, a naturalist. Consider this significant landscape:

> Not all the knives of the lamp-posts,
> Nor the chisels of the long streets,
> Nor the mallets of the domes
> And high towers,
> Can carve
> What one star can carve,
> Shining through the grape-leaves. (C.P. 75)

It affirms the aesthetics of literary Impressionism, with its insistence on visual clarity, the uniqueness of the moment, and hedonistic values. But its refusal of the machine world is quite as impressive as its implied analogy between the machine of nature and the process of the mind. Typical poems of the Impressionist method in *Harmonium* showed how the beholder's mind was dominated by sense impressions from the natural scene, like "Infanta Marina"

> Partaking of the sea,
> And of the evening,
> As they flowed around
> And uttered their subsiding sound. (C.P. 8)

It has often been noted that in the 1921 poem "Nomad Exquisite," Stevens also used a natural phenomenon, "the immense dew of Florida," as a simile for poetic creativity. A closer look at the imagery, however, reveals an antithesis behind the parallelism of the two fecundities, natural and poetic. At the end, the dew turns into flames. This schism of mind and nature widened when Stevens placed his jar in Tennessee and saw it take dominion over bird and bush.

96

WALLACE STEVENS
and the Symbolist Imagination

But he was still conscious of the power of nature, which he variously symbolized as Florida, as the moon, as a maternal archetype. He violently tore himself loose when he wrote "Farewell to Florida" first published in 1934. Her mind had bound him round, he sang, but he was free now, and headed for the industrial North:

My North is leafless and lies in a wintry slime
Both of men and clouds, a slime of men in crowds. (*C.P.* 118)

The shift from the maternal archetype to the figure of a virile hero is documented by many poems of the thirties. What interests us here is that it will eventually deny the possibility of Impressionism. As we move from *Harmonium* to *Ideas of Order,* a constructive principle replaces the symbolism of water and fire, this time to signify without any ambiguity the domination of the external scene by the poetic imagination,

Fixing emblazoned zones and fiery poles,
Arranging, deepening, enchanting night. (*C.P.* 130)

The singer on the shore may well be a woman. What strikes us is the language of masculine power, "the maker's rage to order the words of the sea." The impressionistic verbs of "Infanta Marina," *roaming, partaking, flowing* have changed to the verbs of a new symbolism, a new aesthetic: *to master, to portion out, to fix, to order.*

We have just suggested that this major shift in Stevens' evolution had symbolic, that is to say psychological, roots. We could add that the change from moon-symbolism to a solar cult in many poems of *Ideas of Order* also occurred in Apollinaire's poetry around 1907-1910. In *Les Fiançailles*, which he dedicated to Picasso in 1908, he first compared the moon to a fried egg, then stated that he had given everything except his own shadow to the sun (*o.p.* 134-135). A mental affinity between Stevens and Apollinaire was shaping up. We encounter the first direct borrowings in poems of that period, for instance at the end of "Lions in Sweden":

> If the fault is with the lions, send them back
> To Monsieur Dufy's Hamburg whence they came.
> The vegetation still abounds with forms. (*C.P.* 125)

Ramon Guthrie has established that Stevens' wink at the reader referred to Apollinaire's *Bestiaire* published in 1911 with illustrations by Raoul Dufy. Under the woodcut of a lion, the quatrain reads:

> O lion, malheureuse image
> Des rois déchus lamentablement,
> Tu ne nais maintenant qu'en cage
> A Hambourg chez les Allemands. (*o.p.* 9)

What interests us more than thematic likeness here is the similar *modus operandi*. Both Apollinaire and Stevens confronted the faults of modernity in an aesthetic vacuum. The old forms failed them, and they resorted to ironies until they found a method in Cubist painting. Apollinaire's peacock, spreading his tail, unveiled its *derrière* (*o.p.* 29). Punning against despair, Stevens mixed his vernacular with the demotic French of his confrère, to produce his little bilingual drolleries.

WALLACE STEVENS
and the Symbolist Imagination

Ideas of Order functions as a low-pressure belt in the evolution of Stevens' poetic weather. Impressionism needs the support of nature. It fails in the bleakness of urban winter. New space is a vacuum, the mind is blank,

> The spirit and space
> The empty spirit
> In vacant space (*C.P.* 131)[8]

But less than three years after these discouraged ironies about "The American Sublime," Stevens was able to fill this modern space with an image of himself, or of an heroic self he imagined:

> The poet striding among the cigar stores,
> Ryan's lunch, hatters, insurance and medicines,
> Denies that abstraction is a vice except
> To the fatuous. These are his infernal walls,
> A space of stone, of inexplicable base
> And peaks outsoaring possible adjectives.
> One man, the idea of man, that is the space,
> The true abstract in which he promenades. (*C.P.* 185)

A new buoyancy can be felt here, a deliberateness in confronting reality. At the same time, modern space is removed

[8] Paul Ginestier, in *The Poet and the Machine,* translated by Martin B. Friedman, Chapel Hill, 1961, p. 169, quotes a strikingly similar example of existential anguish caused by space:

> "Je rencontre toujours
> Hors de moi comme en moi
> L'irremplissable vide
> L'incomparable Rien"
>   (Valéry Larbaud)

Obviously modern space must be assumed by a modern consciousness, for its vacuity can be overcome only by speed.

from the "infernal walls" of the city, it is abstracted, like the idea of man, from the materials of industrialized North America:

> From this I shall evolve a man . . . .
>
> At last, in spite of his manner, his eye
>
> A-cock at the cross-piece on a pole
> Supporting heavy cables, slung
>
> Through Oxidia, banal suburb,
> One half of its installments paid. (*C.P.* 182)

It is a far cry from Stevens' modern hero, a telephone lineman on his pole, to Guillaume Apollinaire's triumphant airman, riding his cross to record heights. Unlike Apollinaire's syncretic airplane of Icarus and Eucharist, Stevens' mixture of Greek and Christian mythology underscores ironically the shabbiness of the scene:

> Ecce, Oxidia is the seed
> Dropped out of this amber-ember pod,
>
> Oxidia is the soot of fire,
> Oxidia is Olympia. (*C.P.* 182)

Apollinaire, singing in the Orphic tradition alive in French poetry, took modern man's future divinization for granted. Stevens' Yankee Adamism was less sanguine. At best we shall inhabit Olympia, not Olympus.[9] But underlying the difference was the common belief that art could make the idea of man "A substitute for all the gods" (*C.P.* 176), that by the artist's will,

[9] The distinction was made by John Enck, *Wallace Stevens: Images, and Judgments*, Carbondale, Ill., 1964, p. 128.

WALLACE STEVENS
and the Symbolist Imagination

> L'homme se divinisera
> Plus pur, plus vif et plus savant .... (*o.p.* 174)

Our central contention that the painters' example switched both poets to a style of modernism will now have to be borne out in terms of their aesthetics. The first and perhaps the most important document of the history of Cubism was Guillaume Apollinaire's *Méditations esthétiques*, published in 1913, then run in *The Little Review* in the early twenties, before appearing as *The Cubist Painters* in 1944 with illustrations from Walter Arensberg's collection. There are many, many theoretical agreements between Stevens and Apollinaire: about the limited social function of art ("Continually to renew the appearance nature has for the eyes of men," *c.p.* 13); about the nobility of the imagination, which Apollinaire called its sublime quality; about the split between perceived reality and conceived reality, which Stevens called simply reality and the imagination. But because we deal with two poets who wrote on art as poets, it is undesirable to separate theories from the rich imagery that supports them. *The Man with the Blue Guitar* plays in the same key as *The Cubist Painters*.

Picasso had taught the poets that art begins by destroying the object. Of him Apollinaire wrote that he studied the object "as a surgeon dissects a corpse." Perhaps he meant a pun on the French for still-life, *nature morte*. But Stevens literally took the scalpel to *his* object, the idea of man:

> Ah, but to play man number one,
> To drive the dagger in his heart,
> To lay his brain upon the board

> And pick the acrid colors out . . .
> To nail his thought across the door,
> Its wings spread wide to rain and snow,
> To strike its living hi and ho,
> To tick it, to tock it, turn it true. . . ." (*C.P.* 166)

The metaphor recalls, of course, the bird nailed by Pennsylvania farmers and French peasants across barn doors, a reference also used by Apollinaire in "Le hibou":

> "Mon pauvre cœur est un hibou
> Qu'on cloue, qu'on décloue, qu'on recloue.
> De sang, d'ardeur, il est à bout.
> Tous ceux qui m'aiment, je les loue." (*o.p.* 30)

The vowels in French reverberate the owl's hoot, while the consonant 'k' in both poems gives rhythmic support to the savagery of the action. But the comparison must stop with texture. The themes of the two poems differ radically and in a rather revealing way. Apollinaire bemoans the fate of the Orphic poet, whose greatness derives from his sacrificial suffering. This *sparagmos* with varying degrees of pathos constitutes the tradition of Baudelaire's albatross, Mallarmé's swan, Cocteau's eagle, Eluard's phenix. Orphism is the key to understanding the imagination of modern French poetry. The key unlocking Stevens' symbolic world is Adamism, which Roy Harvey Pearce rightly calls "the Continuity of American Poetry." The subject of Stevens' poetry is "man number one," Adam nailed like an eagle on display. The poetic act is not self-sacrifice but savage purification. The difference between French Orphism and American Adamism hinges on this question: who speaks? Both speak for man,

WALLACE STEVENS
and the Symbolist Imagination

but one speaks as a young god, or angel, the other speaks as common man.

Process is the very essence of modern art. It is an act of savage decreation. Stevens questioned the use of the word "destruction":

> Is this picture of Picasso's, this "hoard
> Of destructions," a picture of ourselves,
>
> Now, an image of our society?
>
> Things as they are have been destroyed.
> Have I? Am I a man that is dead
>
> At a table on which the food is cold? (C.P. 173)

The answer is no. Decreation is not destruction,[10] because art decreates the created only to promote the idea of man: "Modern reality is a reality of decreation, in which our revelations are not the revelations of belief, but the precious portents of our own power" (N.A. 175). Apollinaire had put it more succinctly: "Each god creates in his own image; and so do painters" (c.p. 10). The rise of Cubism was the rise of a modern hero: the decreator.

The opening lines of *The Cubist Painters* give us an insight into the birth of that hero: "Les vertus plastiques, la pureté, l'unité et la vérité maintiennent sous leurs pieds la nature terrassée." Which Lionel Abel translates by "keep nature in subjection" (c.p. 9). The image is more telling in French. Nature, like some feminoid monster, is kept under

---

[10] The original phrase by Picasso was "horde of destructions," which Stevens quotes more accurately in "The Relations between Poetry and Painting." The next quotation, from Braque, balances and cancels out Picasso's: "The senses deform, the mind forms" (N.A. 161).

foot by some virtuous, virile, and veracious Knight. Picasso and Braque are heroes who re-enact the dragon-fight of their individuation. Underlying the Cubist aesthetic is the heroic fabulation with its symbolic triad: *a monster*, nature or reality, *a hero*, painter or poet, and *a flame*, the intense fire of creative subjectivity: "Enormous flame. A new man, the world is his new representation" (*c.p.* 17).

Stevens' evolution from the Impressionist aesthetics of *Harmonium* to the modernism of *The Man with the Blue Guitar* followed a similar pattern. Poem 16 was, in Stevens' own paraphrase, "the stubborn and constantly repeated rejection of the image of the earth as mother."[11] Then poem 19 metamorphosed the earth into a stone monster and confronted it with fierce intelligence:

> That I may reduce the monster to
> Myself, and then be myself
>
> In face of the monster, be more than part
> Of it, more than the monstrous player of
>
> One of its monstrous lutes, not be
> Alone, but reduce the monster and be,
>
> Two things, the two together as one . . .
>
> Being the lion in the lute
> Before the lion locked in stone. (*C.P.* 175)

This is a modern poem because, in resemblance with a Cubist picture of the analytical period, the process of art itself is its subject. It is a crucial poem because it shows a

[11] Wallace Stevens, *Mattino domenicale*, edited by Renato Poggioli, Turin, 1954, p. 178. (Not reproduced in *L.W.S.*)

heroic self replacing all the previous feminine figures of creativity. But it is crucial also because it goes beyond the Cubist aesthetics of conflict between nature and artist to a theory of their conjunction. We measure Stevens' progress and his distance from Apollinaire by the frequency with which, in his later poetry, he will celebrate the marriage of masculine imagination with feminine reality. He wanted to "play of the monstrous lute as its intelligence" (*C.P.* 175) to discover the reality of nature rather than invent it, to "lash the lion, caparison elephants, and teach the bears to juggle" (*C.P.* 385), and these quotations suffice to show how he swerved from the Cubist aesthetics. But it would be unreasonable to deny that the Apollinaire–Picasso example played a role at a decisive time, a role in revitalizing not only his aesthetics but his symbolism as well.[12]

Now we must ask about the validity of these findings in respect to the history of style. But we need a multitude of observations to correct our intuitions. We can only sum them up briefly: In Impressionism, as represented by Apollinaire's *Rhénanes*, Stevens' *Harmonium*, and Monet's late pictures, manner is the result of a tension between the individual signs, paint flecks, or words whose "edges clash" (*C.P.* 13) and the thematic viscosity of the picture or poem. The natural subject matter thus dominates the artificial or naturalizes it. The grammatical object of the verb *I paint* becomes the subject at another level. Illusionistic tendencies

---

[12] Already noted by John Enck, *Wallace Stevens*, who wrote: "Stevens here seems to be bent on outdoing the Cubists, particularly Braque, in breaking up the continuity of surfaces" (p. 124).

are bent on satisfying the body senses with hedonistic values. The symbols of earth, river, vegetation, liquid light, constellate in the maternal archetype which seems central to the Impressionist project. The painter or poet fixes the ephemeral in an attempt to stop time. The euphemization of death by intimations of repose and bright colors motivates the Impressionist imagination.

Opposed to this vision, which probably had a compensatory role for the generation of artists preceding Stevens and Apollinaire, another structure underlines the rise of Cubism and its practice as an aesthetic and moral philosophy. In *The Man with the Blue Guitar*, in the *poèmes-conversations* of Apollinaire, in the prose of Gertrude Stein, the manner manifests a complete shift of the imagination; to summarize it, I shall base my structural model on the paintings of Picasso dated 1908-1910. Their manner depends on a tension between the uniformity of primary signs (the greys, the geometrical forms) and the thematic discontinuity (broken forms, dissociated space). This angular morcellation was of course an influence of the later Cézanne, just as the uniform signs and low iconicity can be ascribed to the influence of Seurat. But Cubism is nonetheless the first "modern" style, by its treatment of the machine-made object. It erupts into the formerly naturistic paint world and disrupts it: collages and flimsy constructions. The first observers of the movement—Apollinaire, Reynal, Salmon—made no mistake: this meant a new idea of man, an idea based on the non-imitative, non-illusionistic feats of the painters. The unconscious values of Cubism are ascetic: purity, effort, and a

WALLACE STEVENS
and the Symbolist Imagination

constructive heroism. A brand-new theory of perception is at work. Like Husserl's eidetic reduction, it builds on Bergson's energizing of sight by memory, but supersedes the Impressionist eternization of privileged moments by a series of *Abschattungen*, which multiply perspectives and extend time. To instantaneism succeeds simultaneity. Death is symbolically ignored by the Cubist, whereas it obsessed the Impressionist. Intelligence rather than the senses becomes the artist's chief tool of inquiry, and like a blowtorch it cuts out the heterogeneous forms of a new reality. A reality not of perception but of conception, as Apollinaire said. The poet instinctively found the symbol for Cubist art: the flame. Solar symbolism paradoxically is at the center of those grey- and brown-hued pictures. The pictures of the Impressionists are not solar, although sun-drenched, because they obey a passive convention of an almost photographic kind. The solar values of creativity place the Cubist artist as Promethean hero at the center of the modern world. The Cubist *askesis* of shedding iconic conventions is a purification ritual, whose biological function may be to recapture man's lost power over time. The importance of art "as a substitute for all the gods" dates from "Les Demoiselles d'Avignon." Instead of the Impressionist merging of subject and object, we have the Cubist logic of conflict and this dualism reverberates at the semiological as well as the symbolic and psychological levels. *The Man with the Blue Guitar* includes most of these characteristics.[13] The syncopation of the rhap-

[13] For a perceptive analysis of formal resemblances between the *Calligrammes* and Picasso's Cubist pictures, see Renée Riese Hubert, "Apollinaire et Picasso," *Cahiers du Sud*, No. 386 (1966), pp. 22-27.

sody, the commonplace language, the preference of sun over moon, the masculine imagery, the discovery of the hero, all these belong. But it evolves toward a logic of noncontradiction and announces another chapter of Stevens' development.

[1968]

5

Poetry and Alchemy

Everything, the spirit's alchemicana
Included . . .

("An Ordinary Evening in New Heaven")

Total grandeur of a total edifice
Chosen by an inquisitor of structures
For himself.

("To an Old Philosopher in Rome")

BEFORE considering the alchemical imagery of Wallace Stevens and following its evolution through his poems, it may be well to remind ourselves of important truisms. Here are three:

1. Symbolic structure is at the root of all thought.[1] Images have their own logic and there can be no question of classifying them according to pragmatic copies of perception, but rather according to the symbolic motives of the imagination. This motivation is found to be either cultural or psychological. Wallace Stevens offers a special interest in these researches because he did "poematize" his own imagination.[2] For him, "Poetry is the subject of the poem."

2. The psychological motivation is summarized in these words: poetry creates the poet. By his images, by the new forms which he invents, he accomplishes a self-creation, at times a self-cure. This is what Wallace Stevens means when he says: "Poetry is a cure of the mind."

3. The cultural motivation is ambiguous because the poet gives more, perhaps, to his age than he receives. He assimilates such images as he can use for his own metamorphosis. At the same time he creates history, at least cultural history, by his writing.[3] History does not explain the imagination, since history itself has to be imagined.[4] But the creative

[1] Gilbert Durand, *Les Structures anthropologiques de l'imaginaire*, Paris, 1961, p. 21.

[2] I am risking the neologism because the poetic act is not a poeticization of that which is already a poem. The world can be poeticized, but poetry is poematized.

[3] For a brilliant and sustained demonstration of this idea, see Roy H. Pearce in *The Continuity of American Poetry*, Princeton, 1961.

[4] It is necessary to distinguish historical myth from existential reality,

WALLACE STEVENS
and the Symbolist Imagination

power of the image extends from the poet to the public. "Poetry helps men to live their lives."

Of these three definitions of poetry, the second especially (the idea of self-transformation) will help us to understand the function of Stevens' images. As for their structure, we will rely on comments which Stevens made in certain hyper-lucid passages, like this extract from "Notes toward a Supreme Fiction":

> Two things of opposite nature seem to depend
> On one another, as man depends
> On a woman, day on night, the imagined
>
> On the real. This is the origin of change.
> Winter and Spring, cold copulars, embrace
> And forth the particulars of rapture come.
>
> Music falls on the silence like a sense,
> A passion that we feel, not understand.
> Morning and afternoon are clasped together.
>
> And North and South are an intrinsic couple
> And sun and rain a plural, like two lovers
> That walk away as one in the greenest body. (*C.P.* 392)

Here we have, in focal tryst, the three axes of Stevens' symbolism meeting at a moment of heightened self-realization, connotated by the line "A passion that we feel, not understand." If we can imbue ourselves with this system without undue intellectualization, if we can feel the development of Stevens' poetry as a long sexual metaphor—a man, a woman, love—then perhaps this poem will have led us to the heart of the body of symbols which he called "the

as Durand did in his treatise, *Les Structures anthropologiques,* pp. 421, 424.

greenest body." But at the same time as the symbolic mode of thinking generates its own heat, passion, feeling, a text of cool awareness invites some diffidence, perhaps inscribed in the hypothetical verb "seem" of the first line. This is what makes Stevens a supreme modern in the French style, the eye of "seem" trained on the copulation of symbols. But we shall bracket this voyeuristic grammar while busy with the symbolic *hieros gamos* of Stevens' poetry. His attitudes to symbols evolved in mesh with the psychological realities which generated the symbols.

Man Depends on a Woman

The drama of Stevens' development, in synopsis, would read somewhat like this: Act One, the poet sings an interior paramour, his "infanta marina," "the One of Fictive Music," whose world is an artificial paradise. But She grows dangerous and is sequestered. Act two, in response to Her threat and the pressure of reality in the 1930's, the poet sings a hero and leans toward abstraction. Act three, She surfaces again from the depth of suppression, and the poet projects a mystic marriage between his abstract giant and the Penelope-image. Act four, beyond the imagination's sex.

The first "act" of Stevens' poetry, continuous from the earliest Harvard poems through most of *Harmonium,* evokes in the majority of readers the sensations of a lush though lucid incarnation, a feel for shapes and colors summarized by Stevens' dictum: "A poet looks at the world as a man looks at a woman." (*O.P.* 165) Susanna bathing in "Peter Quince at the Clavier" recalls the warm and verdant atmos-

WALLACE STEVENS
and the Symbolist Imagination

phere of Tintoretto. Stevens definitely does not begin with
the ascetic nudity of a snow man,[5] but with the more
hedonistic nudity of a beautiful woman. Yet the green color
of the scene, the very substance of happiness, sustains a
natural bond between beauty and death.

> The body dies: the body's beauty lives.
> So evenings die, in their green going. . . . (*C.P.* 92)

Here the imagination of Wallace Stevens is already showing
its livid roots: the biographical facts confirm that, very early,
Stevens was obsessed with death.

> Death is the mother of beauty, mystical.
> Within whose burning bosom we devise
> Our earthly mothers waiting, sleeplessly. (*C.P.* 69)

Having become feminine, instead of the idiomatic masculine,
"Death" receives the attributes of Hecate: the willow, the
fruits, and the leaves of the great underworld mother. Of
course Stevens rejects this myth like all the others. His
rejection of repose in the warm intimacy of the bosom he
indicated by "sleeplessly"; he knows that this maternal
death owes us life: "we devise our earthly mother"; he
places "earthly" and "mystical" in opposition. The arche-
type of the bosom here inverts the significance of the tomb.
Everything in "Sunday Morning" that pertains to the body,
to vegetation, to color, to nourishment, produces an appeas-

---

[5] Nothing could be more wrong than to take "The Snow Man" as a
"point of departure for the luxuriant cycle of the seasons in *Har-
monium*" (Macksey, in *The Act of the Mind*, Baltimore, 1965, p.
195). The first moment in Stevens' perception is not the unmediated
vision of a winter world. Besides, as Northrop Frye put it, "art begins
with the world we make, not the world we see" (*The Educated
Imagination*, p. 23).

ing and euphemizing effect. The descent of the doves, so slow, so undulating, breaks the final fall; the image of the island simultaneously signifies solitude and involution; thus the ambiguity of "Sunday Morning" is the very ambiguity of the maternal archetype: life and death, terror and beauty.

The majority of the poems of *Harmonium* follow this example; the poem about the burning candle at night, the grave of Badroulbadour, the death of a soldier in autumn, the moon, "mother of pathos and pity," the feminine night, "fragrant and supple," and many others carry us into a nocturnal constellation where the diurnal poems, "The Snow Man" or "Gubbinal," appear as aberrant stars. The organizing nuclei of this symbolism constellate between them: mother/death/beauty invokes death/controlled night/color and death/controlled night/music. Mother/vegetation/Florida and mother/boat/vessel are linked by the exoticism of night voyages.

If we wished for a quantification of the feminine symbolism in *Harmonium*, we could muster a spate of words for each one of the functions psychologists ascribe to the archetype of the Great Mother.[6] Such a word-count has value only through comparison between large segments, and the contrast between *Harmonium* and the subsequent collections of Stevens' verse is the significant proof that in the first phase of his development "man depends on woman," while in the second phase this is no longer true. At any rate, and for whatever objectivity it may give to my hypothesis (man *seems* to depend on a woman), here is that array of words:

[6] I derived my categories for the word-count from Erich Neumann, *The Great Mother*, second edition, New York, 1963, pp. 39-53.

The World of Harmonium
(and corresponding poems of O.P.) [7]

masculine			feminine

<pre>
              masculine | feminine

man 54   (but hero 2)   human 11
father 1   child 8   woman 10
sun 46   love 26   mother 19
                                                    moon 53

day 22   night 55

light 18   dark 33

eye 37   blue 40   green 54
            white 28   black 45
            gold 20   purple 14

mind 15   voice 13
think 44   speak 21

                                     music 27
                                     wind 50
                         make 72   poem 15

air 25   sea 57
fire 10   water 41
                                                    earth 22

                                  bloom 27
                                       leaves 31
                                 grow 20 fruit 18
                                     tree 32

            frost 8   spring 15
winter 8 snow 12 cold 13   warm 7   summer 18
            north 7   autumn 12

            rise 5   fall 34

                                                    death 12
                                                    die 42
                                                    dead 10
</pre>

[7] Based on Thomas F. Walsh, *Concordance to the Poetry of Wallace Stevens*, University Park, Pa. 1963, modified by Mrs. Anne Jourlait working under a Rackham School of Graduate Studies grant from the University of Michigan. Their help is here gratefully acknowledged.

As an indication of a major symbolic shift between *Harmonium* and the second phase of Stevens' development (*Ideas of Order, The Man with the Blue Guitar, Owl's Clover, Parts of a World,* roughly 1935-1940) the parallel evolutions of the diurnal cluster and its nocturnal opposite make a rich pattern indeed:

	sun	hero	winter	blue	moon	woman	summer	green
Harmonium (21.5% of the total number of words)	46	2	8	40	54	10	18	54
phase two (33%)	100	49	32	84	57	35	43	51
phase three (*Transport to Summer & Auroras of Autumn,* 35.5%)	72	9	24	68	36	68	51	45
phase four (*The Rock* 9.9%)	30	2	7	7	9	8	12	11

The most striking variations in the table concern the birth of the hero and the concomitant perturbations in Stevens' symbolic sky. This secures my thesis of the psycho-symbolic

WALLACE STEVENS
and the Symbolist Imagination

evolution of Stevens' poetry against claims that changes in
it were only stylistic.[8]

Stevens inherited from the Romantics (Coleridge) and
post-Romantics (Laforgue) the notion that the moon was
a mother symbol. Indeed, anyone going through his letters
for biographical clues would detect an early addiction to
moonlight.[9] *Endymion* is the most cited work of poetry in
Stevens' readings before 1914. He put himself in line with all
the famous lunologists by addressing "his yearly couplet" to
the night star, mother of Jesus and protector of the poets.

But in 1922 Stevens became aware of an evolution. In his
long self-analyzing poem "The Comedian as the Letter C"
he sketched the two great axes of his imagination: one up-
ward diurnal movement and one downward nocturnal move-
ment.

> Thus he conceived his voyaging to be
> An up and down between two elements,
> A fluctuation between sun and moon,
> A sally into gold and crimson forms,
> As on this voyage, out of goblinry,
> And then retirement like a turning back
> And sinking down to the indulgences
> That in the moonlight have their habitude.
> But let these backward lapses, if they would
> Grind their seductions on him, Crispin knew

[8] See my article in *Études Anglaises* (September 1959), "Le thème
du héros dans la poésie de Wallace Stevens."

[9] L.W.S., 1) Letter 48: "a great affection for moonlight," 2) Let-
ter 150: "Rose and gray/Ecstasy of the moon," 3) Journal entry, item
114: "some Queen . . . a noble lady." 4) Letter 176: "the emotions
replace the intellect."

> It was a flourishing tropic he required
> For his refreshment. . . . (*C.P.* 35)

Here begins the steady decline of the moon until its virtual eclipse in the last poems. The reasons? Beyond the anti-romantic attitude, we detect a fear of psychological regression. Now, in 1922, Stevens finds danger in the descent toward the Moon-Mother. She is not the concrete and lofty star of the nocturnal sky, but the dweller in a comfortable hollow. Her "indulgences" turn into the trap of her "seductions," and "retirement" into "backward lapses." Here we have the first evidence that Stevens' moon symbol stands for the feminine part of his unconscious, and already presents a threat to the unified Self. In alchemy, also, the Moon is down and within, while the Sun is up and outside. C. G. Jung advanced the theory that Sol and Luna were the alchemists' celestial personifications of their conscious and unconscious minds, symbolic terms which poets instinctively re-use when speaking of their spiritual journeys.

Thirteen lines above these allusions to his *anima*, Stevens mentions a mysteriously "sequestered bride" (*C.P.* 34) who reappears, it seems, in another 1922 poem, "O Florida Venereal Soil." The title puns on the relation between earth, dirt, and sexuality, a theme carried forward by "convolvulus," "lasciviously," "insatiable," "tormenting." The death theme is suggested by buzzards, undertaker, corpses. Florida has become to Stevens a figure of deep repulsion in which even Freudians recognize the triple Hecate.[10] She takes three forms. The first is the Venus Libitina, tormenting the poet with

[10] This was suggested to me in a conversation with Charles Mauron, author of *Des Métaphores Obsédantes au Mythe Personnel*, Paris, 1963.

WALLACE STEVENS
and the Symbolist Imagination

her insatiable sexual demands; to this funereal mistress
Stevens would prefer the ravished bride of the preceding
poem, Persephone enthroned as an idol in the depths of
night. The last stanza addresses her as the Lady of the
Plants,

> Donna, donna, dark,
> Stooping in indigo gown
> And cloudy constellations.
> Conceal yourself or disclose
> Fewest things to the lover
> A hand that bears a thick leaved fruit,
> A pungent bloom against your shade. (*C.P.* 48)

In this moving prayer Stevens cites the sensual icons which
give protection against fear, the fruit and flowers of Ceres.
Thus aestheticism and euphemization are the two sides of
the poetic talisman.

If we can draw conclusions from this analysis, it seems
that Florida offered Stevens a rich symbol of the different
faces of his unconscious. This interpretation attributes a
considerable importance to the poem "Farewell to Florida,"
which begins the second period of his work. The 1935 edi-
tion of *Ideas of Order,* opened on a "curiously fatigued"
poem.[11] "Sailing after Lunch," in which the symbol of the
boat allowed Stevens to make a rare confessional remark:

> My old boat goes round on a crutch
> And does not get under way.... (*C.P.* 120)

---

[11] The expression is from Louis Martz's pioneering essay, "The
World as Meditation" in *Wallace Stevens, a Collection of Critical
Essays* edited by Marie Borroff, Englewood Cliffs, N.J., 1963, p. 137.

In 1936 Stevens purposely replaced this symbol of a paralyzed libido by that of a high ship plunging on through the darkness. He had just undergone a long crisis and had overcome his inner enemy, the Moon.

Winter and Spring, Cold Copulars

Between 1914 and 1924 Stevens had published, on an average, ten poems yearly. In 1925, 26, 27, 28, 29, 30 not a single publication. At the end of these six years of silence Stevens' metaphors have changed almost radically. It was a transformed man who wrote "Farewell to Florida." A crisis must have taken place. The analysis of the second period of Stevens' imaginative creation, from 1932 to 1942, supports this hypothesis.

A ship under way, the shedding of a serpent's skin—an old image of renovation—darkness, fog, the violence of waves, all these elements indicate a difficult but complete transformation. The tone has changed. The images have suffered a profound conversion, and the antithetical structure of the poem marshals them into two hostile columns:

South	North
the mother moon	men
vegetation	dirt without leaves
permanent summer	winter
nature	the city
music	chaos
death	energy

WALLACE STEVENS
and the Symbolist Imagination

Surely in 1922 and 1923 a few poems of *Harmonium*[12] had already expressed disgust for the South and an aspiration toward the North. But now the evolution seems to have come to an irreversible end. It was no longer a question of swaying between moon and sun but an attempt to free himself of the paralyzing feminine presences which the moon symbolized. "Her mind has bound me round. . . . Her mind will never speak to me again." Stevens feared some danger of death. It comes through the words "sepulchral south," "trees like bones," "ashen ground." The word wilderness even suggests a particular horror of sea weeds. Charles Mauron says somewhere: "dans sa tentative d'auto-création, l'artiste risque plus ou moins la folie. Ses rapports avec la folie sont ceux du marin avec la mer. . . ." But at the same time the sailor needs the ocean. Stevens does not get away from the ocean, since it would mean abandoning poetry. He only changes his direction. He says farewell to the feminine unconscious and enters the world of the mass man where men are just like the waves of the ocean. This transition from the feminine night-realm of the image to the masculine day brings about an atmosphere hitherto unfelt in the world of *Harmonium*, the sense of purity and impurity.[13] "Slime" twice repeats Stevens' desire for purification and askesis. The innocent sensuality of *Harmonium* has given way to a male will.

[12] "The Comedian as the Letter C" and "Sea Surface Full of Clouds," besides "O Florida Venereal Soil" and "Banal Sojourn."

[13] However, this feeling was already latent, as we have seen, in "O Florida Venereal Soil."

Stevens' new inspiration acknowledged a double reality and calls for a twofold motivation. First of all we have the carnal and psychic fatigue of a man at the turning point of his life. The Nomad Exquisite has become a slightly queer *Anglais Mort à Florence*:

> A little less returned for him each spring. (*C.P.* 148)

Jung characterized the turning point of man's life as a partial feminization through the invasion of the unconscious. But note: "Most of the time the conscious self rebels against the power of the unconscious and fights its demands." Against the threat of the triple Hecate, Stevens created a hero who assumed all the attributes of solar virility. The feminine image is displaced by the masculine instance of the self. However, a metamorphosis does not destroy all the previous forms. So the singer of Key West is indeed a woman. But her function, the cosmogonic act of putting the world in order, links the images of the poem to the great archetype of King and demiurge. So, the masculine power of Logos at work when her song ended, and the lights in the fishing boats "at anchor there"

> Mastered the night and portioned out the sea,
> Fixing emblazoned zones and fiery poles,
> Arranging, deepening, enchanting night. (*C.P.* 130)

Stevens' invocation to Ramon Fernandez, who in spite of denials[14] *was* the French votary of Classicism, has become

----

14 L.W.S., p. 823: "I did not have him consciously in mind."

WALLACE STEVENS
and the Symbolist Imagination

synonymous with a heroic posture. A logical-magical power separates, cuts clear, orders the feminine words of the sea, "in ghostlier demarcations, keener sounds."

Stevens' "rage for order," a psychological defense-mechanism transformed into an esthetic, encompassed several elements of the vertical imagination announced in "The Comedian as the Letter C." We have just seen its heterogenizing function, also expressed in "Of Hartford in a Purple Light." Masculine light and height combine in it to give the poet that heroic sense of puissance which Bachelard called a "complexe spectaculaire."[15] Out of new images, Stevens constructed a new Self. That he took the images from the archetypes of heroic power forever present in folklore and myth does not in the least invalidate the contention that his was a conscious effort to rebuild his shattered self. The poems of the thirties abound with the forms of his rich solar bestiary: lions, bulls, cocks, and swans, and above them all the eagle, traditional messenger of the celestial will. He is the central symbol of "Some Friends from Pascagoula" and he groups all the marvels of what Bachelard, again, helped us by calling "le psychisme ascentionnel": dazzling wings, nobility, an igneous atmosphere, the morning air fiery and purified. Isomorphs of the soaring spirit, light, purity, and fire constellate with the power of the word. The poem derives from this solar cluster its forceful imaginative unity. Unusual riming, incantatory effects of the strongly accented first syllable, combine with the jazz rhythms into a primitive ritual hardly matched by any other Stevens poem:

[15] *La Terre et les rêveries de la volonté*, Paris, 1948, p. 384.

> Tell me more of the eagle, Cotton
> And you, black Sly,
> Tell me how he descended
> Out of the morning sky.
>
> .   .   .   .   .   .
>
> Here was a sovereign sight,
> Fit for a kinky clan.
> Tell me again of the point
> At which the flight began. (*C.P.* 127)

By superposing this poem upon "Lions in Sweden," we come to understand Stevens' primitivism. Only the primitive still seems capable of feeling the majesty of a heroic image of the Self.

The second motivation of Stevens' hero was cultural. A set of social factors added their pressure to the psychological pulsions, and his poetry became rich, enriched by the poverty of imagination in North America, intensified by the Great Depression of 1929. But if the spiritual need of his age determined a poet to create images satisfying that need, what then explains the fact that Stevens was the only one among the poets of the thirties to rehabilitate the heroic man? (This fact is documented in a book by Joseph Warren Beach, *Obsessive Images in the Poetry of the 1930's and 1940's*.) The answer is perhaps related more to Stevens' personal need than to the demands of society. At the right moment, however, Stevens was able to engage his liberated creative energy in the mêlée of the thirties. In this somber atmosphere the poetic miracle happened: the emergence of a solar world, luminous, blue, airy, and heroic, penetrated by a virile vision, a world on which poetry exerts a purifying *askesis,* a great power of abstraction, antithesis, and denudement.

The ideological project of "Montrachet-le-Jardin" can be summarized in one clear statement, which expresses the central motto of Stevens' second phase: "Man must become the hero of his world." (*C.P.* 261) But the image of the hero is more confused in this poem than in "Asides on the Oboe" which was written in 1940:

> The prologues are over. It is a question, now,
> Of final belief. So, say that final belief
> Must be in a fiction. It is time to choose.

> That obsolete fiction of the wide river in
> An empty land; the gods that Boucher killed;
> The metal heroes that time granulates —
> The philosophers' man alone still walks in dew,
> Still by the sea-side mutters milky lines
> Concerning an immaculate imagery. (*C.P.* 250-51)

Stevens' hero is the abstract man, then, the philosophical man? Perhaps. Yet beyond the ideas, we must revive and feel all the power inherent in the images. Indeed, we find the glass globe in Schopenhauer, where according to Frank Doggett it means pure consciousness. But had not Schopenhauer himself taken up a dream of those other "philosophers," the alchemists, who called *filius philosophorum* the quintessential product of their quest? Their artificial *anthropos* or glorious body acquired the incorruptibility and the transparence of glass during the last operative phase surnamed *albedo, albatio,* or whitening. The purified body

emerged while wet from that permanent water of the phi-
losophers, *ros marinus* or sea-dew, always associated with
the symbolism of birth. This helps to understand the obscure
allusions: "dew," "seaside," and "immaculate." This kind
of rapprochement is all the more justified as the alchemistic
quest pursued the same spiritual goal as the poetry of
Stevens. The purpose was, Jung tells us in *Mysterium
Conjunctionis*, to attain a state of psychic integration. The
union of the unconscious was projected on the chemistry
of metals, personified by the conjunction of the Sun and
Moon, and morally realized by the conciliation of the op-
posites, good and evil. This is the journey taken by Stevens'
imagination:

> How was it with the central man? Did we
> Find peace? We found the sum of men. We found,
> If we found the central evil, the central good. (*C.P.* 251)

For Stevens, the diamond globe symbolized the goal of the
poetic quest, the supreme fiction projected with the faith of
the alchemist in his Great Work, but projected merely, and
not yet accomplished in 1942, when Stevens indicated his
direction.

In an early essay I wrote that Stevens' hero seemed to owe
nothing to Nietzsche's Superman.[16] I now perceive many
deep affinities between them. They breathe the same cold
mountain air. Having gained individuation by their dragon
fight against the moon-woman, they both seek to centralize

---

[16] "Le thème du héros dans la poésie de Wallace Stevens," *Études
Anglaises*, XII (Juillet-Septembre 1959).

WALLACE STEVENS
and the Symbolist Imagination

their beings, so that "hero," "center," and "breath" become the symptom-words of an evolution recorded by their relative frequency, and, most important, their concomitance:

C.P. & O.P.	to breathe	hero	center
Harmonium (21.5% of total)	9	2	2
Ideas of Order (13%)	5	3	6
Man with Blue Guitar (4%)	3	2	2
Parts of a World (15%)	19	44	27
Transport to Summer (21%)	23	7	19
Auroras of Autumn (14%)	16	2	16
The Rock (10%)	14	2	8

It appears from these collocations that Stevens' respiratory passion (he called the air "mere *joie de vivre*" in a letter to Renato Poggioli) expanded at the same time in his development as did heroism and centralization of the self. He breathed his hero to life in *Parts of a World*, a book published in 1942.

The Particulars of Rapture

In *Notes toward a Supreme Fiction* (1942) the mysterious bride returns in full majesty from her sequestration during Stevens' heroic phase. Surely her clandestinity had been broken here and there by brief appearances: "the naked, nameless dame" (*C.P.* 271), "the sensual, pearly spouse" (*C.P.* 222), "the noble figure, the essential shadow" (*C.P.* 223) "everywhere, . . . nowhere to him" (*C.P.* 231). But these were glimpses that made her absence all the more felt. Stevens could not forget Florida. He still must exor-

cize Flora Lowzen, "evasive and metamorphorid," as a figure
of the Devourer, the weaving spider:

> Mac Mort she had been, ago
> Twelve-legged in her ancestral hells,
> Weaving and weaving many arms. (*C.P.* 272)

To love reality is to love the maternal principle, love's
body. Already Stevens had melded his *Esthétique du Mal*
with the Jungian archetype of the masculine unconscious,
the *anima*, but not without some negative traits:

> He had studied the nostalgias. In these
> He sought the most grossly maternal, the creature
> Who most fecundly assuaged him, the softest
> Woman with a vague moustache and not the mauve
> *Maman*. His anima liked its animal. . . . (*C.P.* 321)

"Mauve," it still seemed to him, was a euphemization of
black.

The alchemists projected their desire of wholeness when
they effected in their retorts the chymical wedding of Sol
and Luna, King and Queen, Sulphur and Mercury. Because
"the alchemical operation seems to us the equivalent of the
psychological process of active imagination,"[17] the state of
mind which they sought to attain may give us an insight
into the same process in Stevens' poetry. What the alche-
mists called the *unio mentalis* was often represented pictorial-
ly by a mandala. But the experience itself could not be
described except by recourse to imagery. Jung says of the

[17] C. G. Jung, *Mysterium Conjunctionis*, Princeton, 1963, p. 256.

image of the *lapis,* or philosopher's stone (often alluded to
by Stevens):

> . . . the alchemist's statements about the lapis, considered
> psychologically, describe the archetype of the self. Its
> phenomenology is exemplified in mandala symbolism,
> which portrays the self as a concentric structure. . . .
> Coordinated with this are all kinds of secondary symbols,
> most of them expressing the nature of the opposites to
> be united. The structure is invariably felt as the repre-
> sentation of a central state or of a centre of personality
> essentially different from the ego. It is of numinous nature,
> as is clearly indicated by the mandalas themselves and by
> the symbols used (sun, star, light, fire, flower, precious
> stone, etc.).[18]

This centroversion of the self occupied the third phase of
Stevens' evolution. The co-occurrence of all the symbols de-
scribed by Jung warrants the hypothesis of a likeness between
the poetic and the alchemical processes. The hero's marriage
with a symbolic woman resembles the alchemist's attempts
to mate his animus and anima projected onto sulphur and
mercury.

It is a series of epiphanies, in the course of which a
usually abstract giant unites, or seeks to unite with a carnal
bride. Here she no longer has the disturbing character of
Hecate; she is a vestal prepared for a form of ritual union.
The first *hieros-gamos* is here, before the immensely absent

[18] Jung, *Mysterium Conjunctionis,* p. 544.

effigy of Ozymandias, popularized by Shelley's sonnet on the Nile:

> On her trip around the world, Nanzia Nunzio
> Confronted Ozymandias. She went
> Alone and like a vestal long-prepared.
>
> I am the woman stripped more nakedly
> Than nakedness, standing before an inflexible
> Order, saying I am the contemplated spouse. (C.P. 395)

Nakedness is a limit. The woman so bared is not Susanna bathing, but a symbol of reality, a paradisial image of integrity.

> Then Ozymandias said the spouse, the bride
> Is never naked. A fictive covering,
> Weaves always glistening from the heart and mind. (C.P. 396)

As in alchemy, two opposites are necessary in order to accomplish plenitude: spirit and reality, man and virgin earth:

> There was a mystic marriage in Catawba
> At noon it was on the midday of the year
> Between a great captain and the maiden Bawda
> And Bawda loved the captain as she loved the sun. (C.P. 401)

The limerick celebrates the sensuality of the Earth-Wife:

> Fat girl, terrestrial, my summer, my night. (C.P. 406)

Yet another superimposition and we shall hold the whole symbolic network. The rehabilitation of the nocturnal woman of *Harmonium* is made complete in the prothalamium of a magnificent poem written in 1948, "A Primitive like an

Orb." The orb is the geometric figure of perfection, inscribed in the title, developed by strophic form, the repetitive movement, by the words themselves:

> With these they celebrate the central poem,
> The fulfillment of fulfillments, in opulent,
> Last terms, the largest, bulging still with more. . . .
>
>   It is
> As if the central poem became the world,
>
> And the world the central poem, each one the mate
> Of the other, as if summer was a spouse,
> Espoused each morning, each long afternoon,
> And the mate of summer: her mirror and her look,
> Her only place and person, a self of her
> That speaks, denouncing separate selves, both one. (*C.P.* 441)

The mirror symbol was already present in "Asides on the Oboe" where it represented the heroic Self. ("The glass with a voice.") We have the following structure:

central poem	world
mirror	summer
hero	spouse
(masculine self)	(feminine self)

The poem celebrates the marriage of the ascetic self with the sensual lover—a reunion of the masculine consciousness with the feminine unconsciousness. But the exultation of these images and the joy and the élan with which they are taken up again and again should not obscure the fact of the "as if" which modifies everything. While it may express the

self-doubt of a diffident master of "qualified assertion,"[19]
Stevens' "as if" corresponds to the alchemist's warning that
his experiments were to be understood "tam ethice quam
physice," as metaphors of the soul's Opus.

> As if, as if, as if the disparate halves
> Of things were waiting in a betrothal known
> To none, awaiting espousal to the sound
>
> Of right joining, a music of ideas, the burning
> And breeding and bearing birth of harmony,
> The final relation, the marriage of the rest. (*C.P.* 464)

The predominant style here is repetitive. Not only through
straight iterations, but also by the thematic return of words
meaning marriage and of sounds materializing this return
(burning, breeding, burning, birth) the poem has a cyclic
structure. Not circular: progress is felt. But cyclic by a pro-
found resemblance with alchemy:

> The opus was often called *circulare* (circular) or else
> *rota* (wheel). Mercurius stands at the beginning and
> end of the work: . . . He is the hermaphrodite that was
> in the beginning, that splits into the classical brother-
> sister duality and is reunited in the *conjunctio*, to appear
> once again at the end in the radiant form of the stone—
> a symbol uniting all opposites.[20]

[19] Helen Hennessy Vendler, *On Extended Wings*, Cambridge, Mass.,
1969, p. 32.
[20] C. G. Jung, *Psychology and Alchemy*, Princeton, 1968, pp. 293-
95.

WALLACE STEVENS
and the Symbolist Imagination

Stevens' circuitous grammar and cyclic imagery, predominant in his third phase rather than in the early poetry, bespeak to us the difficulty of describing the numinous experience of the conjunction. There is yet another mystery which a parallel with the alchemical model may help us to penetrate. The third section of *Notes toward a Supreme Fiction* promotes the thesis that "It Must Change." In clear contradiction, it seems, poem IX asserts the good of repetition:

> A thing final in itself and, therefore, good:
> One of the vast repetitions final in
> Themselves and, therefore, good, the going round
>
> And round and round, the merely going round
> Until merely going round is a final good. . . .
>
> The man-hero is not the exceptional monster,
> But he that of repetition is most master. (*C.P.* 406)

Like the alchemical work which operates a profound spiritual change in the artificer by constant repetition of the Opus, "An occupation, an exercise, a work," the circular poems go round and round toward a center, "the gold centre, the golden destiny" projected in "the lapis-haunted air" (*C.P.* 404), haunted by the alchemist's stone, so that the rotation will go on, like a globe,

> Until flicked by feeling in a gildered street
> I call you by name, my green, my fluent mundo.
> You will have stopped revolving except in crystal. (*C.P.* 405)

The metaphorical yoke is borne lightly by this symbol of the Self, possessed at once of the flowing and fluency of a foreign-named world and of the transparent hardness and stability of the paradoxical stone. Both circle and center, repetition and change, fixity and revolution, Stevens' crystal is a symbol for the conciliation of opposites.

Now perhaps we can understand a little differently the reasons why Stevens characterized his third imaginative period with the word "change"; it is a cyclical power of renovation which alters in an important manner the symbolism of the center already found in his poetry. For Stevens the center is not the *mandala* of absolute rest in a mother's lap; it is the never-ending marriage of Ulysses and Penelope, and it is never achieved:

> The center that he sought was a state of mind
> And the Orient and the Occident embrace
> To form that weather's appropriate people
> The rosy men and the women of the rose. (*O.P.* 112)

The rose represents the traditional symbol of the unified personality. But Stevens sees it in the sexual metamorphosis, which is the union of two beings and the duality of the same consciousness. Did he cure his divided soul? Did he build a new self from new images?

Beyond the Imagination's Sex

Three types of poems make up his last collection, *The Rock* (1954). Some, like "The Plain Sense of Things," look back on the great structure that the poems have built, and admit failure:

> A fantastic effort has failed, a repetition
> In a repetitiousness of men and flies. (*C.P.* 502)

WALLACE STEVENS
and the Symbolist Imagination

The pun on "fantastic" underscores the tension between the plain pond and the imagined pond in Elizabeth Park, somewhat like Proust's feeling in the Bois de Boulogne, when the lake is no longer the Lake because Mme Swann is no longer there. Yet, for Stevens, whatever the sense of desecration and the loss of power, when "The effete vocabulary of summer / No longer says anything" (*C.P.* 506), the possible epiphany remains a necessity. A second series of poems in the late collection (*The Rock* and the posthumously published poems which are contemporary with *The Rock*) have a hopeful, or at least suspenseful, mood. They still envision the wedding of Sol and Luna, still make us sense the mystery and majesty of it. The pond again glistens with the desired shape, "sleek in a natural nakedness," and the cyclic miracle happens with the characteristics of the numinous: presence and light.

> And yet this end and this beginning are one,
> And one last look at the ducks is a look
> At lucent children round her in a ring. (*C.P.* 506)

In this beautifully counterpointed poem, "The Hermitage at the Center," repose is found as a final resolution, a reconciliation of the opposites: the presence felt in the center of the ring, like any archetype resulting from the convergence of symbols, remains unnamed, unseen, a void radiating love and light. In his "Final Soliloquy of the Interior Paramour," Stevens projects one last time the feminine presence whose palingeneses have filled, in fecundity or eclipse, his work from beginning to end. She plays her indispensable role in the rounding out of the whole, so that the Self is reunited as two lovers, speaking as one in the first person plural:

> We feel the obscurity of an order, a whole,
> A knowledge, that which arranged the rendez-vous.
>
> Within its vital boundary, in the mind.
> We say God and the imagination are one. . . .
> How high that highest candle lights the dark.
>
> Out of this same light, out of the central mind,
> We make a dwelling in the evening air,
> In which being there together is enough. (*C.P.* 524)

Of poems which constantly affirm the necessity to look for a center within, the most representative are "The World as Meditation" and "To an Old Philosopher in Rome." Fire, a common symbol for "the celestial possible" (*C.P.* 509), links the two poems, completing upward the elemental structure of Stevens' world. (Water predominated in *Harmonium*, air in *Parts of a World*, earth in *Auroras of Autumn*; now fire, the spiritual principle.) Another one of his bilingual puns, "a spirit without a foyer" from the poem "Local Objects," attests to the need to make the Self a focus as well as a center, a place of fire as well as an abode. Stevens desired, but did not attain, "an absolute foyer beyond romance" (*O.P.* 112).

Because the "weddings of the soul," in spite of the poet's "tootings" (*C.P.* 222) eventually won him no spiritual tenure, by virtue of his own denial of transcendence Stevens looked beyond romance, beyond the imagination's sex. The third group of poems in his late poetry, which Roy Harvey

WALLACE STEVENS
and the Symbolist Imagination

Pearce has taught us to read as "a cure of the mind," "beyond human will,"[21] are the admission that if indeed "God is a postulate of the ego" ("Adagia," O.P. 171) then symbolism, alchemy, the search for the lapis of spiritual wholeness, are finally of no service. That, indeed, was a hard lesson to learn. Pearce suggests that it should not have been hard,

. . . hard to hear the north wind again,
And to watch the treetops, as they sway.
They sway, deeply and loudly, in an effort,
So much less than feeling, so much less than speech. (O.P. 115)

because "the 'cure' has been with us, available to us, all the time! . . ."[22] Pearce is thinking of the "kind of perfected relationship of man and his world" which some modern European poets like Jorge Guillén have enjoyed, which I think the Husserlian Cogito leads us to, and of which, Pearce goes on to conclude, "in Stevens' last poems we can only catch a glimpse."

A completely new Stevens appears at the very end of his life, when he has broken the ego's will, erased the Self's projections into marriageable opposites, and is at last able to thrill at the blankness of reality. He had to cure his mind of "the indulgences" of the moon, the encroachments of anima, by a heroic *askesis*; he had to sever and reunite the giant of abstraction with the "fat girl terrestrial," finally to receive the revelation of existential dasein:

21 Roy Harvey Pearce, "The Last Lesson of the Master" in *The Act of the Mind*, and in expanded form, in *Historicism Once More*, Princeton, 1969.
22 *Historicism Once More*, pp. 288-89.

Of Mere Being

The palm at the end of the mind,
Beyond the last thought, rises
In the bronze distance,

A gold-feathered bird
Sings in the palm, without human meaning,
Without human feeling, a foreign song

You know then that it is not the reason
That makes us happy or unhappy.
The bird sings. Its feathers shine.

The palm stands on the edge of space.
The wind moves slowly in the branches.
The bird's fire-fangled feathers dangle down. (O.P. 117)

Quite different from the Snow Man's (no man's) negated
negations, at the end of the mind, the mind is a shining bird,
of gold, of fire, inhuman: a symbol still, but unsymbolized.

[1966, 1970]

Appendix

Further Reading on Stevens and Painting

Robert Buttel, *Wallace Stevens, The Making of Har-monium*, Princeton University Press, Princeton, N.J., 1967. See especially the felicitous sixth chapter, "A Clinging Eye," which sheds new light on Stevens' sensibility before the poems in *Harmonium*, a blind spot in my own limited view. However, one could do even more in the iconographic vein, more with Stevens' own collection of pictures. Buttel's cautious disclaimer of a Cubist influence on Stevens is entirely appropriate in the pre-Armory Stevens (The Armory Show dates from 1913). But my essay on Apollinaire and Stevens makes the claim, I hope, acceptable for the Stevens of the late twenties and thirties.

A Note on Stevens' Personal Art Collection[1]

Thanks to the generous assistance of Holly Stevens, I have in my possession the photographs of thirty-three art works (oils, drawings, prints) in Stevens' personal collection. A certain system, however imperfectly carried out, transpires from his statements about it. Barring the few London and Paris prints of dubious originality which bordered on the trite, as did the current Japanese prints of the beginning of the century, the core of his purchases presented a relative homogeneity. Essentially it was a collection of French land-scapes, painted between 1910 and 1945. The "pearl" of his

[1] This is a translation and adaptation into English of an unpublished text by Françoise Marin. I am indebted to Mme Marin for her contri-bution, based on a careful confrontation of letters Stevens wrote with pictures he bought.

holdings, a drawing by Braque, got no mention in his *Letters,* our main source of information about his taste, and neither did "Dutch Plain" painted by Gromaire, which deserved his admiration. Never directly bought in Paris, all his French pictures were sent Stevens by his agent, Vidal, before World War II, and after the war by Vidal's daughter, Mlle Paule Vidal. Similarly, Doucet, the great Paris collector, entrusted all his buying to his secretary—but his secretary was André Breton.

Although by different generations of painters, Stevens' choices had a common characteristic. They were marginal, if the center at the time was occupied by the Fauves and the Cubists. They were paintings that, in a quiet way, protested against Cubism, Fauvism, abstraction, harking back to Impressionism or returning to Barbizon "reality." In 1910 Bombois, in 1930 Oudot, refusing theory, responded to a public need to keep things together when the Cubists were disintegrating them. This refusal of modern painting was in fact self-contradictory. The "reality" which these painters reproduced so charmingly bears little resemblance to the real "reality" of modern life. Its problems and anguish gave painting a special restlessness, which these landscapes hide or ignore. When Stevens wrote Mlle Vidal that he liked Braque but had a purse for Bombois (*L.W.S.* p. 545) and added later that he liked Braque "in spite of his modern perversions" (p. 548), he sided with Mlle Vidal's questionable views. If he did have a purse for Bombois, in 1947, he certainly had one for Bazaine, Estève, Gischia, Lapicque, or Pignon, whose painting he judged "depressing" (p. 584). These were the true painters of postwar "reality."

Stevens, true enough, was no genuine collector. He bought pictures to enjoy them. To Paule Vidal he wrote in 1947: "Since I am not able to buy many pictures, I want to buy pictures that I like. That must mean, under the circumstances, pictures that please you. The two pictures by Lebasque which your father bought for me are exactly the sort of thing that I like. The Ceria is a delight to me. The Cavailles although it is a little too large, is one of the pleasantest things I have in the house." (*L.W.S.* p. 548).

Henri Lebasque, who was a contemporary of Fauvism, remained close to Cézanne, whom, however, he betrayed by his refusal to give up atmosphere. Something artificial, rather than natural, results from this suggestion of light's presence. Impressionism is quite conscious of the medium, analyzing, deconstructing sight by the conventions of an elaborate system of brushstrokes. On the other hand Céria, whom Bernard Dorival called a "neo-realist," was popular in 1930 because he created a restful nostalgia, in the manner of Corot, at a time of strife and hardship. Stevens' Céria, boats at anchor near a stone jetty, expressed this refusal of adventure.

Jules Cavaillès, Roland Oudot, Maurice Brianchon, all of them born at the turn of the century, represented "a protest of good sense and subjectivity" (Dorival) against Cubism and Fauvism. They painted for pleasure, to enjoy pictures, as Stevens himself put it. They exhibited at the Galerie Romanet's "Les Peintres de la Réalité Poétique," a Stevensian phrase too.

Stevens' only "modern" painting besides the Braque lithograph was a Tal-Coat, the famous original source of "Angel

Surrounded by Paysans." It is, however, not very representative of Tal-Coat's leading style, an interpretation of reality often oriental in its non-perspective and its fluidity. The still life owned by Stevens has a traditional arrangement on two lines along an empty wall. Its charm does not break away from the general tone of Stevens' collection.

"I like things light and not dark, cheerful and not gloomy . . . real but saturated with the feeling and imagination of the artist" (L.W.S. p. 545). Pictures, whether a Mexican scene by La Patellière or a mediocre olive grove by Marchand, were merely starting-points for Stevens' reveries, a new reality not so sharply finished as to impose itself. His resentment against all modern abstraction ("metaphysical painting") gives us a clue to his own form of imagination, too much itself to accept the distortions of major artists, but capable of leaps of its own: promoting the glass vase to the angelic state of beatitude.   —*Françoise Marin*

Further Reading on Stevens and Laforgue

Daniel Fuchs, *The Comic Spirit of Wallace Stevens*, Duke University Press, Durham, N. C., 1963. Since Fuchs thinks Stevens is "a poet who does not have very different phases, as does Yeats" (Preface), no distinction is available to him between the early masks in Laforguian disguise and the later integrations of the Self. However, *The Comic Spirit* is full of felicitous, even if erroneous, phrases such as "To compensate for the lost grandeur there is his own hauteur" (p. 25).

Robert Buttel, *Wallace Stevens, The Making of* Harmonium, Princeton University Press, Princeton, N. J., 1967. Chapter VII, "Dandy, Eccentric, Clown," shows the decisive influence of Laforgue on the pre-*Harmonium* Stevens. He also suggests new, important leads to a reading of *Harmonium*: a resemblance between "Domination of Black" and "Le concile féerique"; between the embroidery motif in Stevens' early work and Laforgue's literary stitches; between "Disillusionment of Ten O'Clock" and "Complainte des Pianos. . . ." On the iconographical method see my introduction to this volume, and p. 89.

Further Reading on Stevens and Symbolism

Robert Buttel, *Wallace Stevens, The Making of* Harmonium, Princeton University Press, Princeton, N.J., 1967: His chapter IV "An Odor from a Star" parallels rather closely my treatment of Stevens and Mallarmé, except that it brings evidence of "influence" at least as early as 1914. Buttel's access to manuscript poems dating before those published in *Harmonium* has permitted him to support with new authority the statement that "the Symbolists made available to Stevens a number of techniques for defining his paradise with immediacy and depth."

Joseph N. Riddel, *The Clairvoyant Eye*, Louisiana State University Press, Baton Rouge, La., 1965: In chapter 5, Riddel went beyond my *ELH* essay on Stevens and the Symbolist imagination by quoting Valéry on the origin of *Fiction*. Much can be done even in Mallarmé with this notion, and because Valéry is so derivative from Poe, Baudelaire, and Mallarmé, a parallel study with Stevens leads to duplication. Riddel's comparison between Valéry's *ideas* and Stevens' *fictions* shows this well: "abstracting beyond nature against abstracting within nature." Thus the opposition between Stevens and Valéry is exactly the same as the opposition between Stevens and Mallarmé.

Further Reading on Stevens' Imagery

Frank Doggett, *Stevens' Poetry of Thought*, The Johns Hopkins Press, Baltimore, Md., 1966, enlarged upon the incipient scholarship of Stevens' philosophical heritage; he went beyond any other author, by concentrating his attention on the stuff poetry is made of, images, not ideas. This study established Stevens' claim as a philosophical poet to affinities between his images and the images of philosophers such as Bergson, James, Nietzsche, Santayana, and—a revelation to me at least—Schopenhauer. Chapter x is a lucid attempt to define the respective excellencies of poetry and philosophy. My question to Mr. Doggett, when I first read his book, concerned the evolution of Stevens' symbols. Apart from the first four chapters, which deal with the imagery in the chronological order of the poems, *Stevens' Poetry of Thought* seems to create a synchrony of symbols where I would prefer a diachrony. Sun, moon, day, music, rock evidence Stevens' philosophical heritage, which Mr. Doggett documented; my own perspective involves their thematic progress and the system they, together, make.

Eugene Paul Nassar, *An Anatomy of Figuration*, University of Philadelphia Press, Philadelphia, Penna., 1965: a very useful repertory of "figures" classed by thematic affinity (the mind, disorder, order, change) and recombined from that "anatomy" into the living organism of the poems ("Peter Quince at the Clavier," "Le Monocle de Mon Oncle," "The Comedian as the Letter C," "Credences of Summer," "Notes toward a Supreme Fiction"). The basic assumption of the book is that "metaphor to Stevens is always evasion" (p. 18), "all analogy is fallacious" (217), imagination a "warping of the real" (35). But we must mind Stevens' caveat about the supreme fiction and the suspension of disbelief: "The poem about Ozymandias is an illustration of illusion as value" (*L.W.S.* 431). The reader who is too attentive to Stevens' dualities may miss the mysterious "final relation" of the symbol, its power of "right joining" (*C.P.* 464): not either reality or the imagination, but both together *somehow*.

Index of Names

Index of Poems

AND ESSAYS BY
WALLACE STEVENS